Endpapers – A detail of the light
wall at Plantation Place – in another
150 years, will British Land have
property interests on the Moon?
The image shows *Farside Terra*. An
enlarged detail of the photograph of
the highlands on the dark side of the
moon, taken from a distance of
1600km by the Apollo 16 astronaut
Kenneth Mattingly, in April 1972.

No Stone Unturned
A History of
The British Land Company
1856–2006
John Weston Smith

Foreword by Sir John Ritblat

 **British Land**

Published in 2006 by
The British Land Company PLC
10 Cornwall Terrace
Regent's Park
London NW1 4QP
United Kingdom

Telephone +44 (0)20 7486 4466
Facsimile +44 (0)20 7935 5552
www.britishland.com

ISBN 10 0-9554406-0-2
ISBN 13 978-0-9554406-0-1

A catalogue record for this book is available
from the British Library

Designed by CDT Design Limited
Printed by Gavin Martin
Set in Baskerville & AG Book

Contents

Foreword
By Sir John Ritblat

In 2006 British Land celebrates its 150th anniversary.

Having been Chairman for 35 of those years, I am delighted to be able to mark the occasion by the publication of this book. It is the work of my long-time colleague John Weston Smith, Chief Operating Officer, formerly our Finance Director and before that our Secretary, who joined the Company in 1971 and is thus admirably placed to record its history.

As is made abundantly clear, property investment is concerned with the long term. Tracing the story of British Land from 1856 onward, we can see how patterns and strategies gradually evolve over time and yet, paradoxically, there have been many occasions when opportunism and speed of response have carried the day. In the property market, continuity of purpose and policy go hand in hand with flexibility and this is strongly evident in the way we have handled our business dealings over the years.

And yet this is no dry-as-dust corporate history. Property is very much an inter-personal affair and this book pays tribute to the many people who have helped make British Land the company it is today. Peppered with observations and anecdotes, it offers a fascinating insight into how the property market works and maps out the distinctive route by which the Company came to enjoy its present pre-eminent position.

November 2006

Prelude

Wind of change – the
climate in which British
Land operated for the first
century of its existence was
a world apart from the
turbulent marketplaces of
today. Like many of the
images in these pages, this
Heath Robinson cartoon
from the inter-war period
(discreetly modified to suit
its new purpose) was
originally used in one of
the Company's award-
winning Annual Reports.

' A steady, small but undeniably
profitable property business... ,

British Land is a property investment company based in London and founded exactly 150 years ago, in 1856. It is only in the past 35 or so years of its history, however, that it has emerged as a leading player in the UK property market. Under the leadership of Sir John Ritblat, a massive £19 billion portfolio is now owned or managed by British Land.

The prospect of business success on such a scale (and across such a broad range of commercial activities) must have seemed unlikely when the Company was founded. The early history of British Land is highly unusual. The Company was one of a number set up at this time with the aim not so much of making profits for shareholders as of enabling people to buy freehold property at market prices and thus qualify for a vote in Parliamentary elections. In the early years of the Victorian era there were severe restrictions on voting rights – women, of course, had no vote at all – and this necessarily had an influence on the outcome of elections. To increase the numbers of citizens who had the right to vote and thus extend the franchise, the freehold land movement came into being. Inevitably it was the Liberal movement that stood to benefit, rather than the ruling Tories.

The simplest way for an individual to obtain a parliamentary vote was for him to show he owned property. Following the Reform Act of 1832 the standard qualification was the ownership of a house with a "forty-bob freehold", that is a freehold with an annual rental value of £2, which was 40 shillings in pre-decimal currency. A number of freehold land societies were set up with the aim of buying large tracts of land at wholesale prices and subdividing them into 40 shilling plots. The plots were sold, thereby conferring the right to vote on the purchasers. These people also needed finance, which they obtained from a mortgage granted by the society, so thrift as well as politics was involved in the transaction right from the start. The outlay required for each plot was some £60 – £70, a very considerable sum in those days. There was a weekly lottery to decide which individuals should have the privilege both of ownership and the grant of a mortgage, which had to be repaid by instalments at the rate of 5 shillings (25 pence in today's money) each month.

The National Freehold Land Society, which was the immediate precursor of British Land, was established in 1849 by two Liberal Members of Parliament: Sir Joshua Walmsley and Richard Cobden, joined a year later by another illustrious MP, John Bright. The Society was not the first of its kind, but no other organisation grew to such prominence or was active on so wide a scale, especially in London. The public first became acquainted with the project through a meeting held on 26 November 1849 at the London Tavern in Bishopsgate in the City of London, where the principal speaker was Cobden. An account of his speech occupied three columns of *The Times* on the following day (see title page). In a key passage, he pointed out that very few people qualified for a parliamentary vote in the counties. He took the example of Hampshire where, according to the most recent census, there were 93,909 male adults above 20 years of age but only 9,223 registered electors – representing less than one-tenth of the male adult population. It was much the same in Sussex, where the male adults above 20 years amounted to 76,677 and the number on the register to only 9,211, being one-eighth of the male adults. In round numbers, of the 16,000,000 population of England and Wales in 1849 there were 4,000,000 adult males and 512,000 county electors; accordingly, only one in eight of the adult males was on the county register. These were the people whose vote decided the structure of Parliament.

Who were the men who founded British Land? Sir Joshua Walmsley (1794 – 1871) was a teacher who later became a corn merchant, and was an early advocate of the repeal of the Corn Laws. He went into politics in Liverpool, becoming mayor, and then was elected as Liberal MP for Leicester. He was founder, president and chief organiser of the National Reform Association and an active supporter of the 40 shilling freehold movement.

Sir Joshua Walmsley MP – schoolteacher, reformer and one of the co-founders of British Land.

Richard Cobden MP
was a vigorous advocate
of extending the franchise
through increased
property ownership.

Having been a member
of British Land's first
Board of Directors,
John Bright MP went
on to become a cabinet
minister under Gladstone.

Before entering politics, Richard Cobden (1804 – 1865) had been a businessman. He began his career as a warehouse clerk in the City of London, later establishing a calico printing firm. He worked to achieve incorporation for Manchester and Bolton, and then joined the Anti-Corn Law League. He was elected a Liberal MP for Stockport in 1841, subsequently becoming active in the campaign to create freehold votes. He was invited to join Palmerston's cabinet as President of the Board of Trade in June 1859, but declined. However, on behalf of the British Government he personally negotiated and signed a commercial treaty with France in January 1860, reducing duties on trade between the two countries.

John Bright (1811 – 1889) joined his father's business on leaving school, and with his brother took over its running in 1828. He travelled widely in Europe and the Mediterranean in the 1830s. On his return to England he engaged in local politics in the Lancashire town of Rochdale, becoming a founder of the Rochdale Reform Association. He too was active in the anti-Corn Law movement and in efforts to widen the number of electors in Parliamentary elections. He was elected as Liberal MP for Durham in 1843 and then for Manchester in 1847. He joined Gladstone's cabinet as President of the Board of Trade in 1868 and was twice in the cabinet as Chancellor of the Duchy of Lancaster.

Cobden and Bright were both radical figures who were very much in the public eye – hence the extensive coverage of Cobden's freehold land speech in *The Times*. They were great Liberal reformers, apostles of free trade, and were particularly prominent in anti-Corn Law agitation. During the 1840s there had been a strong belief in England that cheap imports of food from Europe and the United States of America were being unfairly withheld from the masses. The price of corn – a staple article of diet – was being maintained at an artificially high level in the interests of the great landed owners, who had long been protected by the existing Corn Laws. The repeal of the Corn Laws in

THE POLITICIAN PUZZLED;

OR,

PEEL ON THE RE-PEAL OF THE CORN-LAWS.

1849 was a triumph for the Liberal free-traders and pointed the way towards further reforms. Astute politicians both, Cobden and Bright realized very early on that, to effect change on any significant level, the vote needed to be extended to a much higher number of citizens – hence the formation that same year of British Land's immediate forebear.

When the National Freehold and other land societies first came into being it was hard to say what the Tories liked least – the threat of an increase in votes for their Liberal opponents, the proliferation of new houses or the freedom for the "lower orders" to gain a place on the property ladder and thus get ideas above their station. There were legal difficulties too. Because the National Freehold Land Society was actually a building society, in spite of its name, it was unable to own land and all dealings in land had to be carried on by the directors as individuals at their own risk for the benefit of the Society. This was clearly unsatisfactory and, from 1856 onwards, land dealings were entrusted to a separate organisation, The British Land Company. British Land operated from the same address as The National Freehold Land Society and with the same directors. The formation of this new company was rendered possible by new legislation permitting limited liability for shareholders in companies, meaning that they only were liable to the extent of their investment. If the company went bust owing money to creditors, there could be no call on the shareholders beyond the share capital.

The business of this new company was to purchase land and to resell it on the best terms it could get to any customer who might be willing to purchase. The political impetus, so strong in 1849, quickly disappeared. Indeed a member speaking at a social evening of the building society in 1861 complained that they had lost sight of the original intention in the formation of the Society. He remarked that Mr. Cobden had advocated the land societies mainly with a view to the enlargement of the franchise, but by

As Prime Minister from 1841 to 1846, Sir Robert Peel (seen here in a *Punch* cartoon) made the difficult decision to phase out agricultural protection by repealing the Corn Laws. This action split his party and led to his own resignation, though he remained an MP. His death in a riding accident in 1850 opened the door for men like Cobden and Bright to press for further reforms.

1861 that objective had faded out (changes to the qualification requirements and the removal in 1859 of the property clause had, however, rendered it largely redundant). Henceforward the main business thrust of the Company was definitely towards home ownership, not voting. Indifference to politics, so much bemoaned in the 21st century, has a long history.

And that was that. The political glamour, the excitement and fame of the Company's start were over. The Company had the commercial foresight to protect its estates by a series of restrictive covenants, which limited, for instance, any additional building on individual plots. Even in its 150th year it still enjoys fees for consenting to variations of these covenants. Long after Cobden, Bright and their colleagues had retired from the fray to concentrate on politics – although the original Chairman of 1856, Charles Gilpin, remained at the helm until 1874 – British Land conducted a steady, small but undeniably profitable property business. Unfortunately little more can be said about this long period of oblivion, since virtually all British Land's records were destroyed during the 1939–45 war.

Even so, a few snippets of information have survived – and a bit of controversy. In the 1870s questions were asked about the close interlinking between the directors of the National Freehold and British Land. Corporate governance was already on the warpath even then, and there was a feeling that the more independent the two institutions were, the better it would be for both. After 31 March 1878 the businesses of The National Freehold Land Society and The British Land Company were formally separated, although they were still conducted from the same premises. At this point, British Land repaid all the advances it had received from the building society. The two organisations, now with separate staffs, continued their activities at 25 Moorgate Street (now Moorgate) in the City of London until 1917, the Society being a tenant of the Company.

The final break in their business relationship was caused by a row about the rent paid by the Society. Despite this tiff, the respective staffs continued a cordial relationship up to the time of the merger of the National and Abbey Road Building Societies, which created the Abbey National. It is an odd quirk of history that before joining British Land both Stephen Hester, Chief Executive since 2004, and John Weston Smith (successively Secretary, Director, Finance Director and Chief Operating Officer 1973 – 2006) were senior executives at the Abbey National.

Of the few early records that survived the Blitz, we know that in the 1860s railway extensions added value to some of the Company's land holdings, for example at Addiscombe on the Mid-Kent Railway Company line, where the station is built on the estate. In the 1870s, the Franco-Prussian War affected profits by depressing the building trade and reducing demand for building land – the dividend was in consequence reduced. In 1873, in addition to the ordinary mode of selling land, the directors invited applications for building leases, which was notably successful on the Highbury Estate. By 1879, the dividend was back to a healthy 8%.

Towards the end of the 19th century the Board of Directors, now under the Chairmanship of Sir David Burnett, inaugurated a policy of acquiring income-producing property investments for the purpose of guaranteeing income and stabilising dividends. The threat of taxation of land values contained in Lloyd George's famous budget of 1909–1910 resulted in the Board intensifying this policy. A few years later the First World War broke out, the Company's business came virtually to a standstill, and it was not until the termination of hostilities that the Company was able to pursue its policy of reinvestment of capital in income yielding securities. With the election of Lord Bethell as Chairman in 1929 – he held the position until 1954 – large holdings of Government stocks were sold and the

Lord Bethell, Chairman of British Land 1929–54.

proceeds used to buy retail shops. This type of property investment gradually formed the larger proportion of the assets.

The Second World War dealt a heavy blow to the Company and the rental income suffered considerably. As a result of the Blitz on the City of London, eight buildings belonging to the Company were totally destroyed, and a large number of its properties suffered substantial war damage. During the night of the 29/30 December 1940, the Company lost its headquarters at 67 Basinghall Street together with its strongrooms, which contained all records from the date of incorporation, except copies of balance sheets from the year 1907 onwards and the original Deed of Settlement. For the remainder of the war the Company conducted its business from temporary premises at 36/38 Copthall Avenue in the City of London and also from an out-of-town office in London Road, Reigate. At the end of the war in 1945, British Land relocated to offices at 25 Abchurch Lane, between the Monument and the Royal Exchange.

With the aid of War Damage Insurance, the majority of the damaged properties were restored but virtually all of those that had been totally destroyed were taken over by local authorities in connection with replanning schemes. In 1954, with its centenary year approaching and new offices secured in Lowndes Street, Knightsbridge, the Company reorganised its finances. It bought additional properties and a considerable part of the share capital of another property company, Selected Land. By 1955 the Company owned 1,865 properties, many of them being freehold interests earning only small ground rents. In 1959 The Hale (Holdings) and Derby Investment Holdings were also purchased.

By the 1960s, wholly owned subsidiary companies held portfolios of offices and showrooms, shop properties, flats, ground rents, houses, garages, factories, warehouses and studios. Only with the acquisition of Quadrant House, Pall Mall, in 1961, did

The Blitz of 1940–41 destroyed almost all the Company's early records as well as many of its properties in Central London. In the post-war years British Land itself would be rebuilt from the ground up.

property development become an integral part of the Company's activities. British Land was still a very small property company, however, and it was not until 1963 – more than a century after the Company first set up in business – that gross rental income exceeded £1 million a year for the first time. All this was to change drastically within the next decade.

1

Blowing Away
the Cobwebs

Cleaning the great dome of Stowe School, an image from the 2005 Annual Report. This Report celebrated the conservation work of the organisations with which British Land collaborates on development projects – in this case the Department for Culture, Media and Sport.

'It was a wonderful, unrepeatable time to be entering the property market. Interest rates were low, demand for buildings was high and supply was inadequate…'

The British Land we know today came into existence on 31 March 1970, when the existing British Land Company – still very much the linear descendant of the 1856 original – merged with Union Property Holdings (London) Limited. The combined undertaking had gross assets of £37.5 million and UPH's John Ritblat – now Sir John – became its Managing Director. He at once set the Company on the innovative course that was to take it into the FTSE 100 as a major player in the corporate real estate field. In so doing he completely remodelled British Land's commercial structure and redefined its corporate and financial strategies.

The seeds of British Land's renaissance had been sown some years earlier, in 1958, when John Ritblat, along with another ambitious young businessman, Neville Conrad, set up the Conrad Ritblat agency. Energetic and skilful, they operated at first from a small office at 83 Wigmore Street, London W1. From the start Conrad Ritblat prospered and expanded, and an early success was in attracting Malcolm Cooper, the head of Allied Suppliers, as a client. Allied Suppliers owned the Maypole, Lipton and Home & Colonial grocery chains as well as Pearks Dairies. They had a large number of shops and were constantly enlarging them, selling them, replacing them – this was a marvellous connection for the young agency, and John Ritblat and Neville Conrad took full advantage of the commercial opportunities that came their way.

Beaverbrook, Charles Clore, Jack Cotton, Hugh Fraser, Harold Samuel and Isaac Wolfson were just some of the household names who became active retail clients of the new firm in this fertile period. The decade and a half following the 1939–45 War was a wonderful, unrepeatable time to be entering the property market. Interest rates were low, demand for buildings was high and supply was inadequate in bomb-damaged London. The tight post-war regulation of the construction industry, meanwhile, prevented any risk of a development boom. Personal income tax rates were excessive – 98% at the peak – but there was no taxation at all of capital

Allied Suppliers' retail chains generated much new business for the fledgling Conrad Ritblat agency.

gains and mortgage interest was allowable in full against income tax. Throw in some inflation, so that mortgages were repayable in depreciating pounds while property values rose with the tide, and Conrad Ritblat had the perfect opportunity.

The firm also acted for Sir Maxwell Joseph, a skilful businessman who later became Chairman of the major hotel company, Grand Metropolitan. He had many other interests – he couldn't resist a deal – and one of them was Union Property Holdings. Recognising that UPH was languishing through his inability to give it proper attention, he invited John Ritblat to use Union Property as his entrée into the wider commercial market. In addition to the Conrad Ritblat estate agency, John Ritblat had built up a small group of profitable private property companies, and in early 1969 a transaction was agreed for these interests to be acquired by UPH for a mixture of cash and shares. The arrival of John Ritblat gave UPH the force and direction that Maxwell Joseph could not spare from his other activities. The takeover was completed on 11 August 1969 and at this juncture Neville Conrad left the firm to run his own quoted public company. He would play no part in UPH's eventual acquisition of British Land and the future of Conrad Ritblat – which at this time had over 100 staff – was now entirely in John Ritblat's hands. Indeed, Conrad Ritblat was part-owned by the newly merged British Land for a number of years before becoming completely independent. It has always operated as an entirely separate organization and, like British Land, has grown through mergers; as Colliers CRE, it had a staff of 730 in 2006.

The future Chairman of British Land had begun his own property career in 1952 with the well-known firm of Edward Erdman. In the more leisurely days of the 1950s – without faxes, emails and mobile phones – communication was often by letter and these were generally delivered by hand. Many of the principal players on the property market had offices in Mayfair, within easy walking reach. John Ritblat started out by

Sir Maxwell Joseph, Chairman of Grand Metropolitan and one of the great entrepreneurs of the post-war years.

delivering letters to them, but it wasn't long before he was the one who would be meeting the recipients and doing deals with them.

So what was the secret of his initial success? Property is a very personal business and John Ritblat was and remains highly personable. Very soon his aptitude for property became apparent. He has a vastly capacious memory for people and places and buildings and transactions. The pace and accuracy of his mental arithmetic is prodigious – he has the answer while others are still putting numbers into their calculators. Property is also a long-term business – the land is there for ever – and so memory can be very important. In one deal, when he was bidding for a department store against another buyer, he remembered that many years earlier a previous owner had retained the right to repurchase the store if it ever came on the market. John Ritblat went to the previous owner, bought the right to buy, and thus got the store.

In 1969, however, UPH was still a very small operation. David Cohen was Secretary and Financial Director and John Ritblat's first appointment was Geoffrey Selwyn, who subsequently spent many years as British Land's Head of Tax, later continuing as a consultant. Although British Land was a much larger undertaking, if not an especially profitable one, it did not escape John Ritblat's attention that this Company was struggling. It had lost its driving force due to the death of Albert 'George' Bourner, senior partner of Goddard & Smith, then one of the leading estate agents. In 1970 Jim Slater and Oliver Jessel sold a stake in British Land to John Ritblat and this, combined with help from common directors, enabled UPH to effect a reverse takeover of British Land in a three-for-five share exchange.

In these early days, senior members of the small British Land staff were William Marsh, who went on to complete 50 years as Company Secretary and remained a consultant for a good few more years, and Alan Wilson, Group Accountant and later Treasurer.

British Land thrives on a
continuity of personnel as
much as of purpose. The
team of directors assembled
in the early 1970s – from left
to right Cyril Metliss, John
Weston Smith, David Berry,
John Ritblat, David Cohen
and Stanley Berwin – was
still in place in 1988, when
this photograph was taken
for the Annual Report.

The following year, 1971, John Ritblat became Chairman of British Land and Sir Maxwell Joseph retired from the Board. David Cohen, Financial Director of UPH, served as Finance Director of British Land from the time of the merger until his retirement in 1989. In addition to his financial duties he was also concerned with the Company's housebuilding activities. Also in that year John Ritblat recruited two new colleagues, Cyril Metliss and John Weston Smith, who were to serve the Company for very many years. Cyril Metliss had previously been a senior partner in the chartered accounting firm of Stoy Hayward, and the range of his activities had covered manufacturing, financial services and property development. He had considerable experience too in receiverships and in liquidating unprofitable ventures. John Weston Smith had been Joint General Manager of the Abbey National Building Society and had then widened his financial skills at N. M. Rothschild. David Berry, another early colleague, started as a consultant, then joined the permanent staff of British Land in 1971. He became a director in 1976 and retired in 1998, having built up and then sold off British Land's Australian business.

The non-executive directors were Stanley Berwin, an eminent solicitor and at that time a director of N. M. Rothschild, who was Deputy Chairman of British Land until his death in 1988, and Pierre Lachelin, a director of Hill Samuel who had been a pre-merger director of British Land. He retired from the Board in 1972. Long-serving Stanley Berwin was an outstanding lawyer and his wide experience and wisdom were great strengths for the Board.

For the first few years after the merger the offices of British Land were at 53 and 54 Grosvenor Street, London W1, where the staff formed a closely knit and friendly team. The atmosphere was cordial but the pace was frenetic, as events which are described later demanded. One of the snags of working at Grosvenor Street was that access to its car park was by way of a rather primitive lift. In the early 1970s there were frequent power cuts in the winter months, the result of strikes, which sometimes lasted for hours and often arrived with little warning. Members of staff were well aware of the risk of being stuck between floors to cool their heels and wheels.

In those early days, John Ritblat operated mainly from his office at Conrad Ritblat, located at Milner House on the west side of Manchester Square, London W1. On the north side sits The Wallace Collection, where he is now Chairman of the Trustees. In 1973 British Land moved close by to 35 Portman Square, London W1 and John Ritblat moved there too.

Strategy for action

The company created by the British Land/UPH merger was still little more than a minnow, but very quickly began to swim in deeper ponds. At first, its main assets were blocks of residential flats which were sold off as quickly as possible in order to concentrate on commercial property. The strategic issue for property companies at this time – which was quite unlike the situation in the immediate post-war years – was that the yield on good quality property was well below prevailing interest rates. British Land was in competition with large, long-established companies such as Land Securities, MEPC, Great Portland Estates, Hammerson, Stock Conversion and Slough Estates, which had raised long-term cheap money in the so-called "Dalton" era (Hugh Dalton was Chancellor of the Exchequer) of 1945–47. These loans, together with the equity base of share capital, provided stable funding for their operations over the next three decades and so they had many years of organic growth which gave them pledgeable surpluses and defensive strength.

None of this was available to British Land, as its assets were almost all newly acquired. For John Ritblat's fledgling Company, starting out with enormous ambition but little substance from its small equity base of £13 million, there was no financing inheritance other than £9 million of funded debt. It was clear that building up assets in the portfolio depended on a fresh approach in which opportunism was the key. In order to move forward, the Company had to make and take opportunities wherever and whenever they arose – in UK and overseas property, and in other commercial spheres.

British Land's use of finance had to be equally novel. Though more shares could have been issued, this route held little appeal, for the Company's objective was to progress by creating wealth for its shareholders. That was primarily measured by growth in net assets per share. If more shares are issued the growth in the Company's property values is spread more thinly, a consequence often described as diluting the equity.

The importance of having cash available for purchases has been mentioned. There is also the impact of borrowed money – debt – on a property company. To show how this works, or can be made to work, take two new companies – wonderfully simple, entirely hypothetical companies with no tax or other complications – that might for sake of clarity be called Britishco and Landco. Britishco, on the one hand, has no debt but issues one million £1 shares to shareholders. The other company, Landco, issues 500,000 £1 shares and borrows £500,000. Each company owns property worth £1 million.

Say the market value of the properties rises 10% to £1,100,000. As a result the net asset value of a share of Britishco rises also by 10% to 110p, up 10%. But the same £100,000 rise in the market value of the properties has a very different effect in Landco. The debt of £500,000 does not get any benefit from the growth in property values which accrue solely to the shares, and Landco has only half as many shares as Britishco, so each share has a net asset value per share up 20% to 120p. Landco's fortunate shareholders have therefore seen double the growth in net assets per share, to 120p per share. On the other hand, a fall in property value of 10% would have reduced the net asset value per share of Britishco to 90p, but of Landco to 80p. The use of debt has risks as well as rewards...

Employing debt in this way is usually called gearing. Aptitude in managing debt assumes almost as much significance as the choice of properties. The impacts of both skillsets are clear in British Land's early activities under John Ritblat's leadership.

Fresh initiatives

A search now began for countries where local finance was available at interest rates below property yields, and the Company quickly embarked on developments in Australia, Belgium and France, followed by Holland and Ireland. Unlike the situation that obtained in the British market, in these countries it was possible for property purchases to be self-financing right from the moment they were acquired, and so a portfolio could be built up without a cash down payment. Indeed, because of Exchange Controls then in place it was very expensive to deploy funds from the UK.

The British market offered scope for another method of making money out of real estate in which expertise, nerve and market feel are severely tested – property trading. Trading involves selecting buildings that can be resold in the short-term to earn trading profits, without the expense of financing the purchase for a long time. Trading is a complete contrast with investment, for it is often over the long-term that the best rewards are earned from property. Cynics sometimes describe an investment as a trading deal that has gone wrong but British Land under John Ritblat has been a consistently successful trader. There is no physical difference between a trading and an investment property, but their tax treatment differed and this made it hard to shift between categories; allocation to a trading or an investment subsidiary had to be settled at the time of purchase. Many a property, incidentally, is held as the sole asset in a subsidiary company, so that either the property or the owning subsidiary may be sold.

British Land then embarked on its most significant acquisition to date – Plantation House in the City of London, a building of international renown

because of its links with overseas trade. This 365,000 sq ft office building would have been quite beyond the reach of the old British Land. For years it had been home to the rubber, sugar and tea markets but by the 1970s insurance, commodities, shipping and banking had come to predominate, to be joined by The London Metal Exchange in 1980. Its wide corridors and equally impressive amenities made Plantation Place a regular "walk through" for many City workers and there were numerous professional firms as well as a travel agent, a variety of shops and a selection of restaurants to cater to tenants and this passing trade.

Both in size and scope, and in the philosophy that underpinned its acquisition by British Land, Plantation House was the building that would set the pattern for the years that followed. The route to acquiring it was not, however, a simple matter of a property conveyance and a payment, but was indicative of a new, adventurous approach to the corporate and financial aspects of the property business that would become British Land's hallmark. It all began, quite innocuously, in 1971 when the Company acquired a 30% stake in, and then control of, a quoted company called Haleybridge Investment Trust. Haleybridge owned a number of diverse businesses encompassing joinery in Australia, motor car assembly in Trinidad, housebuilding in France and insurance brokerage in London. All of these were sold, which produced useful cash flows and also provided equally valuable hands-on management experience outside the property market – this was put to extensive use elsewhere, as will be seen.

In addition to these rather fragmented elements, Haleybridge owned a strategic slice, also 30%, of another quoted property company, Regis Property Holdings. Once control of this stake in Regis was secured, British Land was in a position to bid for the remaining Regis shares – a tense time, but the bid succeeded. For it was Regis, in fact, that owned Plantation House, and it was by pursuing this rather circuitous path that British Land gained what was for

Plantation House was a City landmark for generations. Its acquisition in 1971 was one of John Ritblat's earliest initiatives as Chairman of the newly revitalised British Land. Three decades later, part of the Plantation Place development would be sold for £527 million.

many years its premier City of London office building, a prominent investment that by itself raised the Company's profile way above being the owner of a series of relatively minor residential and commercial properties. It was also excellent security for lenders, thus enabling the Company to raise money and stride ahead in building a property portfolio of quality.

The next year (1972) saw further major indications that British Land was emerging strongly from its years of relative obscurity in the property market. Net assets per share doubled, from 84p to 169p per share, and this was tangible proof that the new venture was succeeding. Having taken on board the 365,000 sq ft of Plantation House the Company went on to buy the Croydon Centre, a 600,000 sq ft office complex, and Broughton House, Sackville Street, London W1. Overseas, the Company's Australian developments expanded to comprise over 500,000 sq ft of pre-lets. British Land was also active in Belgium, the Netherlands and France where, in addition to developments in Lille, Lyons and elsewhere, it purchased a 140,000 sq ft office building at 56 Rue du Faubourg St. Honoré, Paris, opposite the British Embassy. The minnow was definitely swimming with the tide.

Wider horizons

At the same time as it was expanding its overseas activities, the Company was pursuing a programme of opportunistic diversification outside the property sector as a way of increasing its income. This was not entirely new, since Union Property Holdings already owned a cinema group, Classic Cinemas; cash flow from Classic's operations and from disposal of some of its well located town-centre properties proved a useful source of funds. The Classic group was sold profitably at an opportune moment in 1971, the deal being concluded between John Ritblat, Lew Grade and Laurie Marsh on a private bus en route to Heathrow. British Land next bought 73.5% of W. Crowther & Sons, which made bricks from the waste material of power stations. This company became an industrial holding

56 Rue du Faubourg
St Honoré in Paris.
British Land began to
expand into Europe from
the early 1970s. As always,
the Company bought
high-quality properties
on prime city-centre sites.

company, yielding substantial cash flows to enable British Land to finance the purchase of high grade but low-yielding properties.

It was unusual for a property company to venture into managing other businesses, although industrial conglomerates abounded. To its existing interests in brick-making British Land added Hardun Bux Holdings, a maker of corrugated paper, and CQC, a manufacturer of sleeping bags and other specialised made-up textiles for the defence industry that went on

to become a winner of the Queen's Award for Industry in 1985. Then there was Gripperrods, makers of those useful strips that hold carpets in place. British Land also bought Investments in the West, a quoted investment trust, as an additional means of accessing promising situations, and acquired C. E. Coates, a small, soundly based banking operation. From time to time there have been profitable forays into film financing, the most notable being the Oscar-winning movie *The Mission* with Robert de Niro and Jeremy Irons.

A different initiative of long-term consequence was the formation of several joint venture partnership arrangements, each one tailored to suit particular opportunities. A key to British Land's success has been its flexibility in adapting to others' needs and aspirations, rather than seeking to make them conform to a set British Land pattern. "Find out what they want and try to give it to them" was the approach. Many businesses which own properties do not exploit their full potential, understandably concentrating instead on their main business purpose. In a joint venture they can enjoy British Land's expertise in property management and property financing while British Land gets access to buildings that are not on the market, and earns fees for its services. In one such venture with Dorothy Perkins, the high street retailer with some 250 shops, British Land bought the 400,000 sq ft Derry & Toms store in Kensington High Street, London. Some while earlier Dorothy Perkins had added the glamorous fashion name of Biba to its activities. Biba had been hugely successful operating out of small shop premises in Kensington High Street and it relocated to the vast former Derry & Toms department store, but in the very difficult economic circumstances of the mid-1970s it had to close. Considered as a property transaction, however, the Derry & Toms acquisition turned out to be highly profitable.

Meanwhile there was a venture with Commercial Union concerning Caxton and Romney Houses, two Westminster office blocks totalling 360,000 sq ft, and

The Mission with Robert de Niro and Jeremy Irons was a highly successful venture into film finance. This Oscar-winning production also took the prestigious Palme d'Or at the Cannes Film Festival.

A doorway to better things – once famous as the headquarters of fashion icon Biba, the 400,000 sq ft of the one-time Derry & Toms store in Kensington proved to be an immensely profitable investment. The panels were designed by the legendary Walter Gilbert.

another on the Avenue des Arts in Brussels to develop a bank building. On the financing side, the Company arranged a ten year £12 million revolving credit, coupled with an issue of shares, with Mercantile Credit.

Net assets per share, having doubled to 169p in the year to 31 March 1972, rose 2.2 times to 380p in the year to 31 March 1973. Total assets were £245 million, having been only £37 million at the time of the British Land/Union Property merger just three years earlier.

The pattern of activity which had been established for the reinvigorated British Land set the pace for 1973, when the entire Dorothy Perkins business was purchased. It continued to be run by its Managing Director David Roxburgh as an independent business unit with minimal interference from its new parent – another British Land characteristic. Meanwhile the programme of overseas expansion, still driven by higher yields on property abroad and by the affordability – and availability – of financing, continued on its course. In 1973 the Company could report that in Australia it had three office buildings in Sydney, two in Melbourne and one in Brisbane, with further developments in hand in Adelaide and in Canberra. It had also taken a 26% stake in Dominion Properties Pty. Limited, an Australian public developer company.

Office development in France spread to Lyons, Lille and Cergy-Pontoise. In Ireland there were two office developments in Dublin, the Setanta Centre (a joint venture) and Cumberland House, providing 360,000 sq ft. The Company bought a 300,000 sq ft office complex in Rijswijk, near The Hague in Holland, and a 28-storey office building in Baltimore, Maryland, USA. In all, overseas holdings totalled 1 million sq ft in 1973, with a further 800,000 sq ft under development. All of this property was locally financed.

At the time, and for ever after, people wondered how a property company with such a small executive staff could so effectively control remote overseas operations? John Ritblat expressed his approach in two

James Wolfensohn,
President of Schroders,
the future Chairman of
the World Bank and, on
one memorable occasion,
John Ritblat's chauffeur.

succinct propositions. The first was that the executive (usually a director) abroad could not ask whether a particular course of action was to be followed – for how could the Chairman, thousands of miles away, know or weigh all the factors bearing on a decision? The second proposition was that he had to be told what was being proposed to be done, and he had a veto, but in practice he never exercised it.

The United States venture came very close to being much larger. British Land had made a bid to buy the Uris Building Corporation, owner of a $700 million portfolio of properties, mainly consisting of offices in New York City. With fixed, low rate, non-recourse, amortising mortgages providing much of the finance, the cash flow from rents, assuming no increase, alone were enough to repay debt within 18 years. National Westminster Bank and Schroders had agreed between them to subscribe for 25% of British Land and 25% of Uris, so the $127 million net transaction was self-financing. Schroders advised British Land, its team being led by its New York President, James Wolfensohn, later Chairman of the World Bank. Each morning during negotiations, Jim Wolfensohn's car would arrive to take the British Land people to Schroders' downtown office. One morning, they were mildly surprised that the chauffeur did not leap out to open the car door for them. They had not travelled far, however, before they realized that the man at the wheel, complete with chauffeur's cap, was none other than Schroders' President – the regular driver was ill!

It seemed a done deal but, the weekend before completion, younger Uris family members persuaded controlling family members to accept an offer 25 cents per share higher from National Kinney, part of Warner Communications. National Kinney was confident that British Land had checked the property assets thoroughly, but missed the real key to the deal which was the Company's careful pre-financing. British Land's completion of the deal had been delayed by the need to obtain shareholders' consent to a 25% increase in the

Executive roles were more clear-cut in those far-off days of the early 1970s, when multi-tasking had yet to emerge as a force for the common good. By 2004, when this Ronald Searle cartoon appeared in the Annual Report, it could be hard to tell where proactive financial management ended and preparations for the Mad Hatter's Tea Party began...

size of its own equity as part of this financing and during this delay it was gazumped and lost the deal. The unfinanced National Kinney found that it had made an expensive mistake, as it could not afford to pay the higher interest rates which the world economic situation then demanded and which British Land's stringent financing planning had anticipated. Disposing of Uris lost National Kinney and its parent, Steve Ross's Warner Communications, something in the order of $25 million.

Yet Uris remains "the one that got away" from British Land. The deal itself was prospectively very profitable, and indeed the distinguished Canadian developer Paul Reichmann stepped in four years later after some Uris buildings had been sold and did very well with the residue of the portfolio. The greater significance for British Land, however, was that the deal would have expanded its capital base with the support of two powerful new shareholders, Schroders and National Westminster Bank. The problem years of the mid-1970s would have been more easily overcome, and indeed the Company would have been able to profit better from the opportunities that the 1970s presented. The Board learned from the experience, and the 1990s recession proved – as we shall see – its greatest springboard.

2

Difficult Times

The oil crisis and its aftermath

Recovery and refinancing

Buying and selling:
the importance of timing

More acquisitions, more diversity

The Drop Lock

Long-term liquidity

An entrée into Broadgate
and Regent's Place

Innovations in foreign exchange

Prophet warning? A sign of the times at Speakers' Corner, from the 2003 Annual Report. He was wrong, as it happens...

'Never meet a banker
without asking for money...'

After three highly productive years, life suddenly became very trying indeed for British Land – as it did for most companies at the time. Late in 1973, the benign economic circumstances that had prevailed since the British Land/UPH merger of 1970 were savagely reversed. The Yom Kippur War and resultant Middle East oil crisis accentuated the inflationary strains already being felt in a worldwide boom. The British Government's reaction hit the property market particularly hard. Commercial rents were frozen and additional, but unspecified, taxation on property was announced; Office Development Permits were curtailed. Added to this damaging mix were high interest rates with the Bank Rate set at 13% to combat inflation. Then there was the demise of the secondary banking sector, a collapse of business confidence and thus demand for space from tenants. On the political front, a protracted miners' strike led to the institution of a three-day working week to accommodate power shortages. Those of mature years may well remember business being conducted by candlelight! There were two General Elections in 1974, the first inconclusive, the second producing a Labour Government with a small majority.

The inability to undertake rent reviews because of the rent freeze made it impossible for buyers or sellers of property to reach sensible conclusions on prices. As a consequence, the market in properties was effectively halted in its tracks and unable to function. Because British Land was such an active trader in the property market, it was particularly affected by this measure. High interest rates took effect immediately, so all bank borrowing became very expensive at a stroke. Nowadays it is possible for borrowers, including house buyers, to obtain fixed interest rates on their loans, so that they are protected from a sudden surge in short-term rates. Usually the fixed rate will be higher than the short-term rate, but paying that higher rate brings certainty for the life of the loan. Rents are a reliable form of income if the tenant is sound, and both

The three-day week –
a time forever associated
with deals by candlelight,
numb fingers and a market
frozen into inanimation by
a desperately nervous and
unstable economy.

borrowers and lenders gain when the payment of fixed interest is covered by rents. In this period of the early 1970s, however, the financial markets were not generally able to provide fixed interest rates by separate instruments (called derivatives) and so British Land was unable to swap floating rate debt for fixed rate debt. In this climate of crisis banks became understandably very concerned both about their borrowers' ability to pay the higher interest charges, and about the values of the properties on which their loans were secured. It was an uncomfortable time for both lenders and borrowers.

These high interest rates – 17% for new long-term mortgage finance, for example – were a severe burden for the Company as its income was effectively frozen; at one point the share price declined to a few pence. Gradually conditions eased, and the rent freeze had gone before the 1975 Report & Accounts were issued, adding some £500,000 to income. More importantly, the renting and the investment markets were functioning again. Nevertheless, this was a challenging time for the quality of the British Land portfolio both in the UK and abroad. The buildings were of high standard and fortunately they were substantially financed by long-term committed bank loans; the banks, meanwhile, had to sit tight as there were no buyers.

By the 1976 Report & Accounts the consolidated revenue deficit was down to £3.9 million, compared to £7.1 million in the previous year. Property sales, higher rents, the sale of the banking venture C. E. Coates and healthy earnings from the industrial and retail subsidiaries had all played a part in this improvement. The recovery continued, and in the year ending 31 March 1977 the revenue deficit was further reduced to £1.3 million. But the damage inflicted on the Company by high interest rates, severe inflation, punitive property legislation and a major world recession now had to be faced. There were large debt repayments imminently due, and financial markets were restive.

Though economic conditions had certainly eased from the worst part of the mid-1970s, this improvement carried its own special menace. It is a well-known axiom in banking that the time to pursue debtors is not when conditions are worsening, but when they start to get better. As a heavily indebted company, British Land had to watch its step. This was a defining point in the Company's history – and it may not have continued very much longer if it had not negotiated its way through the severe cash crunch that came to a head in the second half of 1977.

Every day there were meetings with bankers. In the boom days before the credit crisis, not all loan documents had been as precise or as extensive as the banks would have liked, so there were marathon sessions with lawyers, all of which had to be paid for by the borrower. The consequence was that, the more onerous the new conditions, the harder it became for the borrower to restore stability in its business. British Land took a rigorous view of its obligations, all of which it met, and thus adopted an equally robust attitude in the protracted negotiations. The Company's principal bankers, The Royal Bank of Scotland, National Westminster (now owned by the Royal Bank), Barclays and Lloyds, stood by it in these times and remain its principal bankers today.

At one stage a senior banker to the Company insisted on addressing the Board to expound at considerable length on his bank's view of British Land's financial condition at the time. Very gloomy he was, and he ended by asking whether the Board agreed with his assessment and his grasp of the fine detail.

"Oh no", said John Ritblat. "It's very much worse than that."

He went on to explain where and why – to the great embarrassment of the banker and his team who had missed so much. Strangely enough, they never came to see the Board again!

If nothing else, this episode illustrates John Ritblat's solid grasp of commercial realities, but he also has an undeniable feel for the property market. There is an instinctive element to property – some buildings let easily, others remain empty, some locations improve, others decline. Some buyers don't know what they want but a sensible adviser will deduce what will satisfy their egos or ambitions in addition to more prosaic issues such as size and price. It is often a question of timing – buying when someone needs to sell, selling when someone needs to buy. John Ritblat's antennae are finely attuned to all the nuances, even (or perhaps especially) in difficult trading conditions.

The other side of the property coin is money and that means having cash and bank loan facilities in place ahead of doing a deal. To be able to buy you have to be able to pay, and show you can pay. At an early stage John Ritblat developed financial expertise to match his property skills, cultivating lenders and partners and constantly being aware of shifts in the money markets. Some lenders want to expand their lending, others are over-extended. A canny borrower knows who is doing what, and keeps in with all of them, because yesterday's loser can easily become tomorrow's winner. "Never meet a banker without asking for money" was an early piece of advice for those who joined the Company.

Recovery and refinancing

Nevertheless, British Land had more than adequately demonstrated during a period of exceptionally difficult business conditions that it was perfectly able to help itself. During the preceding financial year property sales realised in excess of £40 million, of which £36 million related to properties in the UK. The outstanding commitment to development expenditure was virtually all fully funded. A joint venture was arranged between British Land and the Dutch property company N.V. Beleggingsmaatschappij Wereldhave that embraced properties in the Netherlands and in France with a gross value at the time of some £50 million, a transaction

10 Cornwall Terrace, overlooking Regent's Park, was British Land's home from 1978 to 2006. Originally the Company occupied the centre section only but, as business grew, the adjoining properties were acquired. After three decades in the care of British Land, the buildings were sold in 2006 for £50.5 million with the prospect of converting them back to residential use.

which opened the way to a reorganisation of the Company's European interests, leaving it free thereafter to concentrate on the financial situation at home.

What was now needed was a set of proposals that would not only improve the maturity pattern of the Company's borrowings, and lower the ratio of debt to shareholders' funds, but also preserve for shareholders the greater part of their existing interests in the valuable freehold portfolio which British Land had so painstakingly created over the past few years. With a mix of a new debenture stock secured on Plantation House, a convertible loan stock and an issue of ordinary shares, the Company was able to retain its properties and move ahead on a sound financial footing. This step provided the base from which much of the Company's 21st century strength and business would be derived.

Of course it was not as simple as these few words might suggest. There were competing claims from various lenders, and one or two predatory investors tried to force through schemes to procure for themselves some of the premier assets. They were defeated. Helped by the banks which continue to be active lenders to the present day, by some well-disposed shareholders, and by other friendly supporters and its own constant and unyielding determination, the Board raised the money. Lenders and investors alike have profited handsomely.

As early as the next year (1978) the Accounts showed that the Company was fighting its way back. It moved to new offices at 10 Cornwall Terrace in Regent's Park, London NW1, where it would remain for the best part of three decades. Typically, both the departure from Portman Square and the arrival at Cornwall Terrace each represented successful property deals in their own right. An oil company took over the Portman Square space at what was then the highest rent in the West End, and that became the "comparable" for many a rent review. At Cornwall Terrace, the Company's initial occupation was as a tenant. Subsequently a long leasehold interest was purchased and then some time later, when values were high, was sold with the

Company taking a lease back. Inevitably, values fell again, and the opportunity was taken again to be long leaseholders from the Crown Estate. As the business expanded over the years, the adjoining four Cornwall Terrace properties were acquired, then finally 20/21 Cornwall Terrace to house the ever-increasing numbers of staff.

Encouragingly, the revenue account returned to a small surplus. Property sales in the year were £29 million and a further £14 million of sales were agreed after the year end. Helped by property revaluations, net assets per share had recovered to 97p. John Ritblat was able to report that the pace of recovery had been considerably more rapid than seemed likely a year before. The Company had sold properties earmarked for sale earlier than expected in a sound market, but against that there was some impact from yet another change in interest rates, which were at historically high but not peak levels.

It was and remains a strength of British Land that it is always ready to sell properties when the time is right to do so, with no attachment to so-called "trophies". It might be that a particular building had gone ex-growth, or had been improved – or rented – to its foreseeable limit, or that some other entity was excessively anxious to own it. It might just be that there was strong unsatisfied demand in the investment market. Or it might be that the Company had better ways to use funds elsewhere.

After the pressures of the 1974–77 downturn, the next period saw a programme of sales to reduce debt, including the Liverpool Exchange Building, Setanta in Dublin and International Buildings in Kingsway, Central London. After six years in British Land's ownership the retailing arm, Dorothy Perkins, was sold to Burtons in September 1979 ahead of a downturn in retail trade. It had provided invaluable cash flow, and the consideration for its disposal was received partly in cash and partly in properties which were integrated into British Land's portfolio or sold. One commentator observed that this was a sensible transaction as British Land was better with property and Burtons better at selling knickers. It certainly was true that some of the properties acquired provided both profits and headaches in equal measure. One of the buildings looked very handsome, until it was realized that the facades were made up of a range of differing sized pieces of glass, only obtainable from abroad and prone to break whenever the sun shone! With such transactions you cannot pick and choose all the buildings...

A British Land development completed in the late 1970s that had some interesting elements was 120 Aldersgate. This was a small 29,000 sq ft office property on the edge of the City of London and close to the Barbican. It included a swimming pool, which also served as the water tank for the sprinkler system. The letting market was still not easy and it took a lot of effort to find a tenant. Finally the Post Office, which in those days also controlled the telephone service, seemed almost persuaded, but then hesitated. It took a well-directed call to a trade union official, warning him that his members might miss out on the swimming pool, to close the deal.

In Australia the Company established a Property Trust in association with the Post Office Staff Superannuation Fund (holding 51%) and the Conzinc Riotinto Staff Provident Fund (holding 24.5%). The Trust satisfied the restrictions that had been imposed by the Australian Foreign Investment Review Board and so British Land was able to continue to invest (the concern then current was that too many Australian properties were being held by foreign owners). The Trust held British Land's developed properties in Brisbane, Canberra, Melbourne and Sydney, with a gross value in excess of A$41 million and comprising some 800,000 sq ft. This transaction produced a cash surplus of A$19 million for British Land and all the floating rate Australian debt was financed on fixed terms.

A decade of achievement

Emerging from the switchback years of the 1970s – initially so successful but latterly so testing – the Company entered the new decade restored and reinvigorated, but still facing difficult UK economic circumstances. Continuing high interest rates inhibited expansion and development, so there had to be ingenuity.

An example of British Land's ever-inventive approach was the imaginative conversion and letting of a 33,000 sq ft floor of the Derry & Toms department store building in Kensington High Street for office use. Originally acquired in a joint venture with the now sold-off Dorothy Perkins empire and then occupied by ICL, it was later let to Visa, the international credit card enterprise. After conversion, Marks & Spencer and British Home Stores became the principal retail tenants of the building. The building also had a large banqueting facility and British Land's chief surveyor was pleased to accept an invitation to attend a reception there. Unfortunately, drifting cigar smoke discovered a shortcoming in the alarm system, causing it to activate more than once during the course of the evening. Developing and owning property is not always plain sailing!

In 1980 the Company was able to report that 81% by value of its portfolio was freehold, up from 67% a year earlier. Dividend payments started again. It was also able to move forward once more through the corporate acquisition route, bidding successfully for the Corn Exchange Company, owner of a desirable City freehold, and the United Kingdom Property Company, with a diversified property portfolio and some industrial businesses as well. These industrial activities, control of which might have deterred other potential pure property bidders, were absorbed into the Crowther division which had the necessary managerial skills. Among the clutch of new companies involved was Beclawat, which made windows and doors for trains, buses and cars, and had operational bases in the UK, Sweden and Australia.

Over the years British Land has has made its mark on London's infrastructure. Developments such as Broadgate, Plantation House and Regent's Place would have a major impact on the built environment, but historic buildings have also found a place in its portfolio. One of these was the Corn Exchange, seen here in Victorian times. It was still in use for its original purpose at the time of the acquistion and the floor of the trading room still had the ribbed floor that had once trapped discarded samples of grain. An interior view of the new Corn Exchange development is seen below.

One of UKPC's assets was Heywood Industrial Estate near Manchester, consisting of large sheds which had originally been built for military use. A building on the site was used for the storage of vast quantities of cigarettes and on one occasion the manager saw a helicopter landing close by. Fearing that the warehouse was under threat, he raced to the site. By the time he reached it the helicopter had taken off, but he managed to take the number. After police enquiry the response was an apology – the pilot admitted he was lost and had dropped down to check his map!

The Corn Exchange Company presented a legislative challenge. It had been established by its own special Act of Parliament, and to move the actual Exchange elsewhere therefore required the tortuous processes of a new private Act. This particular Act was delayed beyond the usual extensive timetable by a General Election – Mrs. Thatcher's second victory – which causes all private Acts to require resubmission. Eventually, with the agreement of the Corn Exchange's traders, who were compensated for moving, British Land's tenacity paid off, the Act became law, and handsome new offices profitably replaced the outmoded exchange buildings.

Each of these corporate acquisitions illustrate British Land's readiness to undertake rather more than just buying chunks of real estate in the conventional way. This willingness to tackle intricacy has paid off on numerous occasions over the years. One such example was the acquisition of Wellingrove Property Investment Company Limited, which had a portfolio of properties which were largely let, with the exception of a crumbling building in High Wycombe. It was a neglected timber-framed building, believed to be the last example in the town, originally known as The Chequers Inn and thought to date from the mid sixteenth century.

Restoration as a timber-framed structure was impossible, as it had been allowed to decay over a number of years. It had been the subject, four years before British Land's acquisition, of a local planning inquiry, which had refused consent to demolish. With the aim of establishing the best way forward British Land therefore held a series of meetings with local restoration societies, the local authority and the relevant government department. As a result of this consultation the relevant consents were eventually obtained. Notwithstanding tempting offers to sell, a facsimile building was constructed, successfully let, and sold profitably. This was an example of how a relationship with the local community can yield a mutually acceptable result. It is known in the market too, and sellers of valuable but complicated assets appreciate that it is always worth trying a deal with British Land.

At the drop of a lock

Despite these successes, the Company still had to proceed cautiously. As high interest rates continued to prevail, cash was both precious and a good earner – £17 million of cash and other readily realisable securities was held at 31 March 1981. A significant financing innovation, however, was just around the corner – one that would deliver tremendous benefits in the following year and indeed for many years to come.

In 1982 British Land completed a Drop Lock Debenture Option secured on Plantation House with a group of UK institutions, giving the Company irrevocable access to £37 million of fixed rate funding in one or two tranches at its choice. Under the Option, British Land had the right to compel these lenders at any time to lend at a pre-agreed margin over gilts. Provided £10 million was drawn by August 1987, the Company had until August 1991 to draw the rest, and the life of the loan was to 2024. If gilt rates fell to stipulated levels, British Land had to take the money (that is, the Drop Lock "locked" in to place) but the cost to it would be below 10% – a wonderful bargain in those days.

The Drop Lock was British Land's "multi-million pound note". All lenders, particularly the banks, would be reassured by the knowledge that there was access to long-term liquidity available to British Land. Happily not one of them ever asked for part of the proceeds to be earmarked for its own loan! The benefit to British Land's credit, nationally and internationally, was enormous. Every seller of property to British Land could feel that it was good for the money and able to pay. The property business is bedevilled by buyers offering apparently juicy prices but "subject to financing" which then does not materialise. A record of reliability as a buyer, allied to speed in paying, gives British Land a real market advantage. The cost of the Drop Lock was modest, at only 0.125% per annum, which was not dear for such long-term access to even longer-term money.

At that time the Bank of England was able to regulate the timing for issuers and borrowers which wished to come to the market, a control which could be very awkward when companies needed funds urgently. However the Drop Lock had been given Bank of England approval, to be drawn at any time during the option period. Not surprisingly, the authorities quickly closed this loophole (it may have been exceptional, but it was still perfectly official) as it conflicted with the regulatory timing process through which money supply was controlled. Fortunately for British Land the action was not retrospective and the Drop Lock's exercisability remained in place. So loans were drawn, the second tranche just before the Option expired, and the resultant Debenture Stocks, until they were refinanced in 2006, remained in the Balance Sheet for many years.

The Company continued to expand its overseas activities in the 1980s. It bought a controlling interest in Growth Realty, a Real Estate Investment Trust (REIT) operating widely in the USA and listed on the New York Stock Exchange. This was 25 years before REITs were permitted to operate in Britain. Separately it acquired 90 Broad Street, New York, a 328,000 sq ft office

The Company's first purchase in the United States was the 250,000 sq ft Arlington Central Savings Bank Building at 201 North Charles Street in Baltimore, Maryland.

British Land accumulated its Broadgate properties in careful stages, as if it were patiently building up a major collection of artworks. The first acquisition was a minor interest in 1 Finsbury Avenue.

building. With the 250,000 sq ft Central Savings Bank Building in Baltimore and shopping centres in Grand Junction, Colorado, and in Palm Springs, California, the American business was now substantial, and was to grow further with Growth's development of two apartment buildings in New York and the purchase of a 282,000 sq ft office building, at 315 Park Avenue South. In Ireland, British Land gained planning consent for a 375,000 sq ft shopping centre at the corner of St. Stephen's Green in the retail heart of Dublin, which was built, leased and later most profitably sold, part in 2001 and the residue in 2004.

An apparently minor note in the 1983 Chairman's statement remarked that the Company had joined a consortium, subscribing for a £34 million debenture with equity, in an office building being developed at Finsbury Avenue, London EC2. This was the first step in the 20-year process that would take the Company to full ownership of the Broadgate Estate, the 4 million sq ft office complex forming the new core of the City of London.

1984 marked the beginning of a different but characteristic British Land process. The renewed growth of the Company after the refinancing was still impeded by high interest rates in Britain. Overseas, however, much cheaper money was available but at the price of foreign exchange risk. Swapping the liability into sterling would merely reinstate the sterling interest rate. By good fortune, contact was established with Neil Record, a former Bank of England economist who had devised an innovative computer-based scheme for managing foreign exchange expenses without risk. It was recognised that the resulting surpluses and deficits would not fit neatly into the then-existing concepts of the UK tax system, impeding the rational offset of profits and losses, but it was felt such a complication did not justify losing the opportunity of tapping a new source of finance.

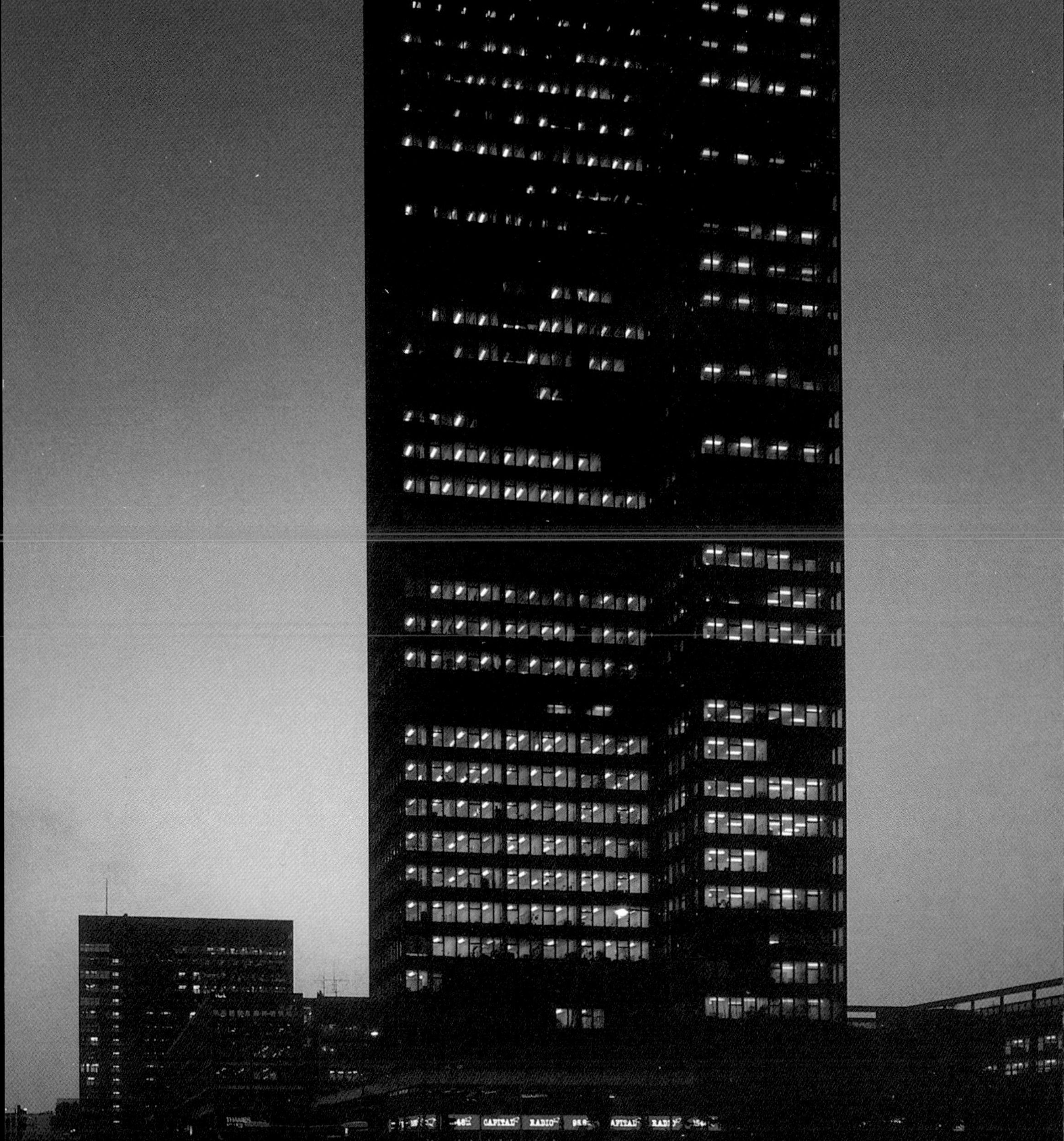
CAPITAL
RADIO

The Euston Centre in the mid-1980s. This tower has not greatly changed in the intervening decades but the offices below it, running along the Euston Road, have altered out of all recognition. This 10-acre piece of nondescript real estate offered British Land a tremendous commercial opportunity, and it is here that the 2 million sq ft Regent's Place is still being developed.

The Company issued a Swiss Franc Bond in May 1984 (followed shortly by a second) and the necessary daily computer monitoring and the entrée into the foreign exchange market added greatly to the Company's range of expertise. In the event, the tax disadvantage was absorbed and the system ran successfully for some years.

That same year also saw the purchase of a half share in the Euston Centre, London NW1. Another public property company, Stock Conversion, owned the other half, and there were those in the market who wondered why that company had not taken up the chance to complete its ownership. Half a loaf may be better than none, but a whole estate is usually preferable to a partial interest – unless of course you spot a bargain, which is what British Land had done. In 1986 it was able to buy out the Stock Conversion share (by that time Stock Conversion had itself been taken over by P&O), and gained control of the Euston Centre, a 10-acre site with 1 million sq ft of office and retail space built in the 1960s. With British Land in control it has proved possible to redevelop the site which will eventually comprise over 2 million sq ft of modern space. It has been renamed Regent's Place in recognition of its proximity to Regent's Park.

3

Back to
the Plantation

Deftness of touch is important
in the property market. During
archaeological digs associated
with the Plantation Place
redevelopment, traditional
pick-and-shovel building
methods gave way to a more
delicate approach.

‘It takes a lot of nerve to judge the moment. Catch it if you can... ’

The City holds many secrets but few have come to light quite so unexpectedly as the hoard of 43 gold coins at Plantation Place. High-value coins such as these – worth around £2,000 each at today's equivalents – were not in everyday use and the accumulation of so many was possibly connected with a business transaction. The example shown below carries the likeness of the emperor Hadrian.

In 1971, the acquisition of the 365,000 sq ft Plantation House had been one of John Ritblat's earliest initiatives when he assumed control of the newly revitalized British Land. For many years it served the dual purpose of being a major provider of rental income and a highly regarded source of security for lenders.

In the 1980s the City of London was undergoing extensive redevelopment and Plantation House clearly offered enormous potential. The Company bought the adjoining freehold buildings at 53 Eastcheap and 34/42 Fenchurch Street, EC3 expanding the site to 2.1 acres. Later it bought Chesterfield House, on the corner of Fenchurch Street and Rood Lane, and later still two other adjoining buildings in Eastcheap. Save for a listed Wren church, this completed British Land's ownership of the entire island site. This process – classically British Land in its gradual evolution over time – opened the way for construction of Plantation Place, some 30 years after the original acquisition. The new development was completed in 2004, with Plantation Place South a little after, together providing some 700,000 sq ft of modern office and retail space. In 2006 Plantation Place was sold by the Company for £527 million, while Plantation Place South remains part of the British Land portfolio.

Plantation House had enjoyed a long run in British Land's hands, producing excellent income until it was demolished and a highly profitable outcome thereafter. During the redevelopment process there was an unexpected cash bonus, when preliminary archaeological surveys of the site uncovered a spectacular find of Roman gold coins in mint condition, bearing the heads of Roman emperors spread over a century. They are now on permanent display at the Museum of London.

Some view developing new buildings such as Plantation Place as the basic task of a property company – the choices of sites and design, the skills of construction and leasing and managing. In strategy, timing is often the key. There are many delays before building can

start. Buying the various land components to assemble a site can take years, as can obtaining planning consent. And there is always the market. Starting to build when everyone else is building may mean a glut of available space and thus falling rents. A sudden rise in interest rates will affect costs. An economic downturn may reduce demand from occupiers. It takes a lot of nerve to judge the moment, especially as a new development will not be available for some time after construction starts. There is a period after a downturn when building costs are lower than in the optimistic days, the empty space is being absorbed and there are few new building starts. Catch it if you can!

A half-term break

At this juncture of our history, approaching the half-way point of the management tenure of John Ritblat and his team, it is a moment to reflect on the techniques that were employed so successfully over the years. The core themes of his stewardship have been:

- a willingness to undertake technically difficult tasks to achieve profitable objectives, for instance by successfully completing not one but two company takeovers in a chain of ownership to secure Plantation House

- using partnerships with other businesses to gain access to property not in the market, for example the joint ventures with Scottish & Newcastle and GUS

- buying into a small stake in an enterprise, gradually expanding the interest as opportunity arises, for example the 20-year acquisition of the 4 million sq ft Broadgate Estate, which began with a participation in 1 Finsbury Avenue. The same waiting game applied to the stages in buying the Euston Centre, now Regent's Place

- buying the Corn Exchange Company and then obtaining a private Act of Parliament to redevelop it and realise the site's potential

- running 120 Classic cinemas, the Crowther industrial group and retailers Dorothy Perkins to enhance income

The ever-changing light wall at Plantation Place by Simon Patterson has become one of the City's most spectacular features.

- venturing abroad when finance and prospects were better than at home, even though the legal and regulatory systems, real estate practices and sometimes the languages were different

- using new financing techniques such as the Drop Lock and Swiss Franc borrowing.

These are examples of his approach to business. But what of John Ritblat the man? He was educated at The Hall School in Hampstead and Dulwich College – later becoming a governor of both. He is a polymath – knowing much about so many fields, able to bring to bear many elements of knowledge, constantly updated on strategy. He absorbs, he retains what is useful and he thinks. As part of this process he is always ready to listen, and then add something else to what he hears. He treats ideas as jewels, to be polished and improved if that is possible, to be gently discarded if not, so that creators will come back to him again with another.

People tend to stay with him for the long-term. He gives and receives loyalty. John Ritblat's long and successful career is based, as might be expected of an outstanding property leader, on wonderfully firm foundations, with a strong commitment to the family ethic, both for his own family and for those around him. His caring greatly for everything and everyone is of a family nature, and his paternalism is reciprocated because it is sustained and so warmly expressed. He has a very extended family and clearly rejoices in it. This feeling of personal warmth and friendship forms the glue that binds his colleagues to him and him to them.

He is a highly sociable creature, always out and about, with an enormously wide acquaintance. It has been said by Max Beerbohm that "we are divided into either hosts or guests" (remarking, incidentally, that no Roman ever was able to say "I dined last night with the Borgias") but this is not a division that afflicts John Ritblat, as he stars in both capacities.

Around him, John Ritblat had assembled a strong and experienced executive. In the Plantation

As a Board member for 11 years Stephen Kalman had particular responsibility for development activities.

Place era the development team was led by Stephen Kalman, who became a director in 1988. Ronald Christie was the long-time Chief Surveyor, remaining in post until 1987, sadly dying only two months after he retired. He was succeeded by Michael Gunston, with John Iddiols as his deputy.

John Iddiols joined the Company when it took over Rank City Wall Limited, owner of a number of office buildings on the sites of former cinemas. On one occasion he took Ron Christie to see a site at Holton Heath in Dorset. The site had a long history, tracing back to the 1914 – 18 war, when it was used as a munitions factory. At one stage they scrambled up a hill to get a good view of the surrounding area. Ronald Christie casually took out his pack of cigarettes, as he was wont to do, and before lighting up enquired as to the nature of the hill. John Iddiols told him that it was locally known as Nitro-glycerine Hill and probably not the best place to smoke a cigarette.

There was a phalanx of accountants – Alan Wilson, Stuart Slack, Colin Stubbs, Tony Adams and Naren Raichura, the latter three still with the Company in 2006. Managing British Land's industrial activities involved many of those who had previously owned and/or run their companies when they were independent concerns – Mark Radiven at Crowther Brickmakers and John Honour at Bux Corrugated Containers being prime examples. Takeovers by British Land did not involve managerial clearout. Rather the view was – and is – that those who know what they are doing are best placed to make money from business, with financial controls and overview management in place, but no nitpicking! Michael Usick undertook the linking management until his untimely death in 1989.

Purely property
By 1986 the Company was substantial, with gross assets of £631 million and with net assets per share of 217p. Pre-tax profits were £21.1 million, having almost doubled over the previous year. At this stage, British

Land underwent a further phase of its evolution. Over the previous decade, its policy of owning freehold or long leasehold buildings, where reversions were continually being realised, had been blended with a rising profit stream from managing a range of financial, industrial and also housebuilding activities (this through Jarvis Brothers and Brewster) and from dealing in properties. Net rental income from properties was more than enough to meet interest charges.

Sales of properties over that decade had exceeded £300 million, producing both profits and resources for new acquisitions of ever-improving quality, fuelling a progressive cycle of expansion from internally generated funds. In 1987 the Group was able to report that gross assets exceeded £1 billion, and net assets per share were up 25% at 271p. Profits were up 423% at £30.1 million.

It was at this point that most of the industrial division was sold, the Company now being able to earn its keep solely as a property company. The cash flow from industrial activities had served the Company well, but to some institutional shareholders there was uncertainty about British Land's identity – was it a conglomerate or a property company? That issue was now resolved, but not without some investor-Jeremiahs wondering whether the Company could prosper without industrial income. The answer was that it could, and did, and does. The Company's share price responded rapidly to the change, rising from 161p at the start of 1987 to 307p six months later.

The focus of the Company was being further refined and the 1988 Accounts reported the sale of the last industrial company as well as the French and Dutch interests. Much of the Company's interests in the former Growth Realty Company, which had been renamed British Land of America in 1983, were sold to Medical Management of America, a Chicago-based company specialising in laser eye surgery. British Land of America was listed on the New York Stock Exchange and Medical Management of America was able to issue its shares to acquire other laser surgery practices elsewhere in the USA. British Land itself retained the two principal New York properties, 90 Broad Street and 315 Park Avenue South, in addition to a continuing interest in MMA.

There was also a strong development thrust in Ireland, where the Company was behind the construction of the prestigious new St Stephen's Green Shopping Centre in Dublin. In 1988, British Land in partnership with the Irish developer, Hardwicke, won the competition to design and build the new International Finance Services Centre in Dublin, better known as the Custom House development. This was a 2 million sq ft phased scheme on a 27 acre site in the heart of Dublin, one of whose features was to be a tax regime that would levy a rate of only 10% on net surpluses. As part of the negotiation with the Irish Government over the Custom House development, an operating licence was obtained, local staff employed and British Land's foreign exchange management was based at the Irish office.

New business was otherwise mainly confined to the United Kingdom, but in the meantime there had been a number of Board changes. Stanley Berwin, long-time friend, solicitor and Deputy Chairman, died on the day after the 1988 Annual General Meeting. That same year Peter Simon, formerly Deputy Chief Executive and the Investment Director of Legal & General, joined as a non-executive director, followed a year later by John Spink, who was very experienced as a chartered surveyor and as Director of Property at Prudential.

In 1989 David Cohen retired, to be succeeded as Finance Director by John Weston Smith, and Stephen Kalman joined the Board as Development Director. Two years later, in 1991, Nicholas Ritblat, who had joined the Company in 1987 after gaining considerable finance experience in investment banking and elsewhere, was appointed an executive director. The executive directors operated as a close team, taking on

different responsibilities as the needs of the business demanded. Thus Cyril Metliss looked after the industrial businesses, but also had a wider commercial role in the UK, Europe and especially Ireland. David Berry, as previously mentioned, had established the Australian business but was also active in UK, and Netherlands developments. John Weston Smith set up the USA venture and was succeeded in the US by Gerald Rothman, who was a director between 1986 and 1988. And John Ritblat was everywhere!

Something new

Property is a cyclical business. The start of the 1970s had seen British Land achieve enormous success before running into difficulties in the horrendous economic circumstances of the decade's middle years. In the 1980s it continued its recovery and was growing rapidly again, to the extent that between 1987 and 1989 net assets per share rose 96%, from 271p to 531p.

By late 1989, however, there were indications that the property market was becoming overly exuberant once more. As John Ritblat observed in his 1989 statement:

"Property markets are likely to face a greater challenge than has been the case over the last few years when growth has been strong and consistent."

Though others ploughed on regardless, British Land saw this challenge as a major decision-point. Having survived the pressures of the 1970s, the Company was wary. It foresaw the importance of liquidity in this climate and had built up over £500 million of committed unsecured bank facilities – and ceased all physical building activity. Such indebtedness as there was – £421 million against gross assets of £1.85 billion – was largely insulated against variable interest rates.

The Board of British Land also foresaw a potential opportunity arising from its own preparedness for a downturn. To maximise advantages for shareholders, it had concluded that the best route forward was to

Right time, right place – in the late 1980s, British Land's far-sightedness led to a number of landmark projects in Dublin, including the development of this new shopping centre at St Stephen's Green.

divide the Company into two by realising the existing, largely freehold portfolio and distributing the cash to shareholders. At the same time, shareholders were to receive an investment in an entirely new "sister" company, named New British Land, to be run by the same management.

New British Land would start out with a strong balance sheet and no contingent capital gains tax liability. It would have a smaller asset base and thus a greater potential for increasing net asset growth at the rapid rate achieved by "old" British Land when it was smaller. The proposals were highly tax efficient. By taking advantage of the Advanced Corporation Tax regime then in existence, the Company could obtain a set-off against its Corporation Tax liability and obtain a tax credit for shareholders. Gross funds also would receive a tax credit in respect of Capital Gains Tax, to which they were not liable.

Initially, this imaginative proposal was widely welcomed, but the British susceptibility to envy concentrated on the prospective benefits for management rather than the immediate advantages for shareholders. For the tax efficiencies to work it was essential that just over 50% of New British Land was conditionally owned by management, and this proved a breaking point, even though some 74% of the management shares were to be subject to a "claw-back" arrangement in favour of old British Land. The claw-back would operate unless old British Land performed at least 4% better than the property sector and New British Land performed at least 20% better, with pro rata entitlements for lesser outperformance.

Outperformance of these magnitudes would of course be highly beneficial to shareholders. They stood to gain immediately from the proposals, which included a tender offer for 10% of the equity at 420p per British Land share, well above the price before the announcement of 300p per share. A holder of 40 British Land shares who took advantage of the tender offer would, had the transaction proceeded, have retained 36 British Land shares and received 13 New British Land shares. The holder would also have received an associated tax credit, which was expected to be one-third of the closing price of New British Land shares on the first day of dealings, in respect of the dividend of New British Land shares. Additionally, by taking up the tender offer for 10% of existing shares, holders would also have received 1680p in cash as a result of selling four British Land shares in the tender offer and 356p of associated tax credit in respect of those four British Land shares repurchased. Moreover, if the performance conditions were not met, holders were to receive further cash and New British Land shares, the amount and number depending on the extent of the performance shortfall.

These certainties, and the attractive prospects, did not succeed in persuading shareholders to withdraw their objections. The proposal could not be altered to offer concessions without seriously affecting the tax structure from which investing institutions were to benefit, and so the proposals were, regrettably, withdrawn by the Board. What shareholders and the market had almost certainly not perceived was that the property market had reached the end of a long boom and was about to move into severe recession. But because British Land had obtained commitments for £500 million bank facilities, had sold an appreciable part of its portfolio and had ceased all development, it was well placed not merely to ride out the recession but to take full advantage of it. Ironically the New British Land transaction had offered investors a unique opportunity to cash in at a peak in the market. By rejecting the transaction, countless policyholders and pensioners of investing institutions found themselves much the poorer.

Recession opportunities
British Land's management team was disappointed by this outcome but retained its drive, and indeed the opportunities which it had foreseen were now actually being provided by the recession. For a cash-rich company these were exceptional. Once more adapting to circumstance, the Company redirected its thrust to the

supermarkets, where market conditions enabled it to invest in long leases – up to 35 years – with minimum guaranteed uplifts at the fifth and tenth years. If prevailing market rents rose above the guaranteed level, and they did in many instances, then British Land was entitled to those higher rents at review. Landlords with funds to invest were scarce, and so the Company could take its pick of strong tenants such as Sainsbury's while paying prices for acquisitions which left room for growth. Indeed in his 1991 Chairman's Statement, John Ritblat was able to state that a general decline in property values had been mitigated in its relative effect on British Land by the substantial volume of new purchases, which had been valued in excess of the prices paid.

No less than 40% of the Group's total rents was subject to guaranteed uplifts as a result of those new investments. Shareholders were assured of a minimum rise to a fixed percentage compounded annually, and amounting to between 30% and 40% at the first five-year review, with a similar uplift at the tenth year. Thus an initial yield of 9.5% could rise to a minimum of say 13% at the fifth and 17% at the tenth year. Some leases had guaranteed uplifts at the fifteenth year too. It was of course a matter of policy to ensure that starting rents were modest, so that growth from those levels would affect rent reviews, if resulting in rents higher than the guaranteed uplifts.

During the downturn the Company was able to add about £900 million of high quality property with excellent potential, nearly all of it freehold and modern, and on terms which were not achievable at any time during the previous decade. In addition to the large retail acquisitions there were substantial purchases at 1, 2 & 3 Finsbury Avenue, Broadgate, where previously only a minority interest in 1 Finsbury Avenue had been owned. Profits were again moving upwards after two years of decline in 1990 and 1991, and it was possible, as the Chairman stated in 1992, to look forward to a selectively improving trend.

At Broadgate, as much aesthetic importance is attached to the spaces between the buildings as the fabric of the structures themselves. Its squares and colonnades were laid out as places where people could relax and enjoy themselves, and it became home to one of the largest open-air art collections in the country. In the foreground of this view from 175 Bishopsgate is the five-ton bronze statue of Venus by the Colombian artist Fernando Botero. The building on the right, Hamilton House, would later be demolished and replaced by 10 Exchange Place.

The Quantum Leap

In his time Sir John Ritblat has pulled many a fine plump rabbit out of his hat, none to more spectacular effect than the acquisition of Broadgate, where this sculpture by Barry Flanagan graces the Arena.

'...the best bargains often become available in the years of recession, when others are forced to sell. '

Late in 1992 the Board embarked on a carefully targeted drive to seek a major joint venture with a partner who would be prepared to invest in the Company and enter into profitable co-investment with it. British Land had emerged from the recession relatively unscathed because it had the foresight to have in place the precautionary measures described in the previous chapter. A briefing document was therefore prepared that would explain the Company's strategy and demonstrate to potential investors exactly how the Company had evolved since 1970 and how it was preparing for the future.

John Ritblat ensured that the illustrious investor George Soros, who was well known to him, had sight of the document early in 1993. This persuaded the great financier that involvement in the real estate sector, and with British Land in particular, would be beneficial for his Quantum Fund, which had a record of highly profitable investment over many years. Once the briefing document had been studied, Quantum Fund executives agreed to make available up to £250 million for investment through The British Land Quantum Property Partnership (BLQ), and in addition subscribed for 11.3 million British Land shares, being 4.8% of the existing share capital.

Having Soros and the Quantum Fund on board was a huge advantage. It represented a massive step forward for British Land, which at the time had gross assets of under £2 billion and net worth of £833 million. Under the terms of the partnership, acquisitions by BLQ were to be financed equally to the extent of £250 million each by British Land and Quantum, making a total ungeared fund of £500 million. As a substantial entity in its own right, BLQ could expect to raise its own finance through the banking and capital markets and thus increase its purchasing power. British Land was paid to manage BLQ, although investment decisions required agreement between the parties. British Land, however, retained the ability to be sole investor in activities which might impinge on the

George Soros

value of its existing portfolio. In parallel with these arrangements and to fund part of British Land's investments through BLQ and elsewhere, the Company made a fully underwritten rights issue to raise approximately £132 million.

The effects of this venture were electric. British Land's share price, which had stood at 179p at the end of 1992, had risen to 436p by the end of 1993. The whole Quantum deal would not of course have been possible if the Company had not anticipated and protected itself from the worst effects of recession earlier in the decade. British Land Quantum had brought tremendous firepower to the acquisition process, and the flow of transactions offered was enormous. Properties bought at this time included the 733,000 sq ft Eastgate Shopping Centre in Basildon, Essex, and several Tesco superstores as well as 122 Leadenhall Street in London EC3, an 181,000 sq ft City of London office building. The partnership also bought 51 Eastcheap, an 81,000 sq ft office building adjoining Plantation House. The alliance lasted for less than two years before, late in 1994, an opportunity arose to buy out the Quantum interests in the partnership. It had been envisaged from the start that British Land would eventually become the ultimate owner – property ownership and development is, after all, its primary purpose – but there was surprise that the option should be exercised while the British Land Quantum Partnership was still relatively young. Because British Land had itself provided the finance to gear up the partnership, using its extensive unsecured facilities, the buy-out only involved a payment of £142 million, though the partnership – including British Land's existing share – had gross assets of £600 million.

In the 1994 Report and Accounts the Chairman's statement recorded that over £1.6 billion had been spent on purchases in a concerted bid to provide a thoroughly modern and diversified portfolio. Out of a total portfolio that now stood at just over £2.2 billion, 72% had been acquired in the previous five years – the best bargains often become available in the years of recession, when others are forced to sell. With values falling and little in the way of competition from buyers who were anything like as well resourced, British Land could enjoy a period of intense activity buying good quality, well located buildings at very attractive prices.

The executive responsible for acquisition during this very active period was Jamie Ritblat, John Ritblat's younger son. He was at British Land from 1990 until 1996, when he left to run his own company. He and his brother Nick, who left in 2005 to set up his own property venture, brought an added dimension to the Company – at one time they comprised 40% of the British Land five-a-side football team.

Nor was financing neglected. In 1993 alone, the Company raised over £500 million in the long-term capital markets, including £166 million of new equity, £200 million from the issue of a 35-year domestic debenture, and £150 million from a 30-year unsecured Eurosterling issue. In addition, it exercised its option to exchange £115 million convertible bonds into capital in the form of preference shares. Much of this funding was swapped in the international capital markets, so that interest rate and currency exposures could be managed independently of funding sources and matched to the business with maximum cost-effectiveness and flexibility.

By the end of the financial year ending 31 March 1995, the Company was able to report that its portfolio had risen 54% in the year by £1.2 billion to £3.4 billion in value, following the most active year the Company had yet seen.

Broadgate and beyond

Other significant moves in 1993 and 1994 related to the Company's growing interest in elements of the Broadgate Estate in London EC2. In 1993, the Company had increased the existing partnership to 100% of 1, 2 & 3 Finsbury Avenue, at the western end of the estate. The next year it was able to arrange for BLQ to acquire a

29.9% stake in Stanhope Properties, which in turn owned 50% of Broadgate Properties. There followed the purchase of control of Stanhope Properties and therefore the assumption of its bank debt which was overdue for repayment. This intricate and extensive transaction brought British Land control of Stanhope's 50% shareholding in Broadgate Properties, which was the owner of some 2 million sq ft of prime office buildings at Broadgate and Ludgate within the City of London.

Broadgate had been developed in a joint company (Broadgate Properties) owned by Stanhope Properties, led by the developer Sir Stuart Lipton, and Rosehaugh Properties, controlled by financier Godfrey Bradman. Their joint company had also developed the Ludgate

The Rt. Hon. Margaret Thatcher, Prime Minister, at the inauguration of construction of Broadgate phases 1 & 2, 31 July 1985.

estate, which formed part of the assets obtained by
British Land. However, the recession had weakened
both Broadgate Properties and Stanhope, while
Rosehaugh went into receivership. By 30 June 1995
Broadgate Properties had external indebtedness of
£795.7 million and in addition shareholder loans of
£127.1 million, with a net equity of only £117.9 million.
There was a loss for the year of £14.4 million.

Clearly, refinancing by a financially powerful
owner was desperately needed. This was not an
insuperable problem since the principal assets, being of
high quality, could support substantial debt. For British
Land, there was a great deal of attraction in having six
buildings providing approximately 1.5 million sq ft of
offices within the Broadgate estate (1 – 2 Broadgate,
4 Broadgate, 6 Broadgate, 135 Bishopsgate, 199
Bishopsgate and Exchange House) and three further
buildings totalling 500,000 sq ft within the Ludgate
estate (1 Fleet Place, 10 Fleet Place and 100 New Bridge
Street). The prospect from EC2 was soon to become
more enticing still since, within a matter of months,
British Land was able to buy the remaining half of
Broadgate Properties. The deal involved negotiations
with over 100 banks and, when it was done, the Group
portfolio had risen to £4.4 billion.

The interval between the Stanhope purchase and
the buy-out of Broadgate Properties was almost a year,
a nerve-wracking period as there were other prospective
buyers in the wings showing a keen interest. The
legal issues were exceptionally complex, with many
participants, there was a constant threat of litigation
and some of the investors and bankers involved were
more than a little intransigent. But this was also a period
which, as the Company had foreseen, would see a rapid
decline in interest rates. In consequence British Land
was able to cover the cost of interest on the price paid
out of rents right from the start. Paying for the various
purchases cost over £1.3 billion. The Company raised
£150 million through property sales, and profitable ones
at that, along with £222 million from shareholders in

The eastern edge of Broadgate, looking out across Exchange Square with Exchange House on the left and 175 Bishopsgate beyond. In the foreground, the massive basalt figures of Xavier Corbero's family group stand sentinel.

a 1 for 6 placing, £250 million in a 40-year mortgage debenture, and some £700 million of new bank facilities.

As part of the Broadgate acquisition the Company had also secured control of Broadgate Estates Limited. This subsidiary company had been formed in 1986 to provide building and estate management for Broadgate itself. Under the energetic leadership of its Managing Director, Barry Winfield, it expanded its remit to provide services to a wide range of external clients, in the City of London and elsewhere. A profit centre in its own right, the Broadgate Estates team undertakes building commissioning and acceptance, maintenance, security, cleaning and property accounting for some 5.6 million sq ft of office and retail space, the majority of it for independent owners and occupiers outside the British Land Group.

Like much of British Land's activity both before and since, buying Broadgate had been a long planned strategy that had evolved over a decade and more. The Company had first become directly interested in the Broadgate site in 1982, taking a stake in 1 Finsbury Avenue. Nine years later, in November 1991, it obtained 100% freehold ownership of numbers 1, 2 and 3 Finsbury Avenue. However, it took until 15 January 1996 for the whole of Broadgate Properties to be acquired and, as we shall see, there were further additions to the Broadgate portfolio in later years. With hindsight, perhaps the most remarkable aspect of the Broadgate story was the way the Company anticipated and responded to changes in both interest rates and tenant demand. Out of the 2 million sq ft acquired by 1996, the Broadgate element was fully let and only 61,000 sq ft was still available to rent at Ludgate.

More joint ventures

It was not all offices, however. In a new departure, British Land entered into a £200 million joint venture with Scottish & Newcastle in 1996 in order to buy 306 pubs let to The Chef and Brewer Group (a wholly owned subsidiary of Scottish & Newcastle) and which were mainly located in the South of England. The venture, named the Public House Company (always known as "Pubco") entered into new leases with Chef and Brewer that had an average term of 25 years for each property. Scottish & Newcastle guaranteed the rental payments.

As the year progressed, the Company moved still further down the joint venture route. Late in 1996 it added a £175 million joint venture with Tesco to which both parties contributed retail portfolios. Then early in 1997 it formed BL Universal, a £960 million joint venture with Great Universal Stores. Each of these joint ventures had its own financing. The BL Universal portfolio contained 982 separate properties, primarily in high street shops, and British Land's retail asset team became fully engaged in exploiting the portfolio's potential.

And then there was the Custom House Docks Development in Dublin, to which reference has already been made. By 1998 the eleven-year programme was in its final stage in conjunction with the Irish Government and Hardwicke, the Company's Irish partner. The Company had developed and sold over 1 million sq ft of office and retail space, 333 apartments, a 235 room hotel and parking for 2,000 cars on this 27 acre site that had been transformed from dereliction.

The dot.com years

To pay for the Company's expanding range of activities, new sources of finance were now needed. A major development in the debt market was the introduction of securitisations, which provided debt related to specific cash flows from assets but without the rigidity of the long-term debenture market.

The Broadgate Estate was ideal for this purpose, with high quality tenants in prime, well located real estate in the City of London, and in 1999 British Land raised £1.54 billion in its Broadgate securitisation. Access to the rated securitisation market lengthened maturities and reduced costs. This was by far the largest financing it had ever done and exceeded anything else that the market had seen. There was a range of maturities extending out to 2038 with significant flexibility to make earlier repayments.

In late 1998 the Company had expended £800 million in adding, in addition to the Broadgate buildings it already owned, 100 Liverpool Street and 155 &175 Bishopsgate, thereby catching a dip in the market which had been rattled by a putsch against President Gorbachev in Russia and the failure of Long Term Credit Management in the United States. As a result British Land was able to buy these highly desirable buildings, which added to its securitisation pool at an opportune time, at yields of around 7%. The funding cost of the securitisation just a few months later was 6.15%.

The property market is cyclical and, as has been remarked, the best opportunities to buy often arise when it is unsettled, as was certainly the case at the time of these purchases. In March 1998 the Company had recorded an annual uplift in City of London values of 13.6%. At March 1999 the annual uplift from a difficult year was only 1.9%, but the deals were there to be done, and on a yield basis that was highly attractive – the level of interest rates then permitted financing at levels below the property returns provide by these prime assets.

This was a time when the fundamental attractions of property briefly went out of fashion, so far as stock market investors were concerned. Bedazzled by the dot.com bubble, they allowed themselves to believe that the old rules under which investors looked for growth in assets or trading potential (and thus profits) no longer applied: all one had to do was to pile into the new technologies and enormous rewards would be forthcoming. For a while stock prices rose rapidly, but

in the end the old economics reasserted themselves. Surprisingly quickly the dot.com bubble ended, as all bubbles do, in staggering losses for investors. British Land was affected by the euphoria in its early stages, when the share price rose above 800p in March 1998, though the net asset value was only 594p per share at the time. This was clearly unsustainable and apparent – the dot.coms' misty hopefulness was not. By February 2000 the British Land share price had declined (perversely perhaps) to 327p, while the net asset value had risen sharply to 594p per share by 31 March 2000. The psychology of the market is not the subject of this history!

A major counter-cyclical event in this period when property briefly went out of fashion was the Company's acquisition in 1999 of an extremely fashion-conscious investment, the Meadowhall Shopping Centre near Sheffield. This 1.3 million sq ft development, with over 200 retail stores on a 125-acre site, serves a catchment area of 7.5 million people within a 60-minute drive time, has two points of access off the M1 motorway and is only 3 miles from Sheffield city centre. It also has its own railway station, is on the Sheffield Supertram network and is accessible by over 80 bus routes. Since British Land acquired Meadowhall, rental income had risen from £45 million per annum to £81 million by 2006. The original purchase cost, including liabilities assumed, was £1.17 billion, and the Centre services a securitised debt of over £850 million.

With Meadowhall clearly promising good things, the following months saw a concerted attempt to extend the Company's retail base through a strategic move with another property company, Liberty International, which was the owner of several leading regional and super-regional centres. British Land reached a conditional agreement with Standard Bank of South Africa which would have made British Land a 29.9% shareholder in Liberty. The £515 million offer was a careful mix of cash and, at British Land's option, British Land shares. The deal involved some complicated technical issues

Shop till you drop – the acquisition of Meadowhall in 1999 anticipated the 21st century retail boom, with British Land almost doubling its rental income inside seven years.

but, unfortunately, the Bank itself then became the subject of a bid, as a result of which it became necessary for it to hold an Extraordinary General Meeting to obtain shareholder approval for the disposal of its Liberty stake.

Regrettably, this could not be obtained. The potential target's board was not enthused at the prospect of a 29.9% holding in British Land's hands and some investors expressed concern at the rapid pace of growth pursued by British Land at a time when the stock market emphasis was resolutely, if unwisely, fixated on the dot.coms. So it was just as well that British Land had the foresight to insert break-fee provisions, which contributed a useful £16.6 million to the year's pre-tax profits and made up for some of the disappointment the Company suffered. But when the results for the year ended 31 March 2001 were announced with a net asset value per share of 802p, the share price had recovered considerably and again exceeded 500p. The thrust into retail properties was pursued further, with the purchase of 22 Homebase stores adding a further 865,000 sq ft. The Company also bought London & Henley, which owned 758 apartments primarily in Central London, in continuation of a policy of residential property development and investment which could be activated whenever good opportunities arose.

Changes at the top

There were changes on the Board both in the late 1990s and in the early years of the 21st century. Bob Bowden, Head of Property Investment and Acquisition, became an executive director in 1997. In 1998 Shen Adam, Managing Director of Broadgate Properties, joined the Board but remaining only until 2001 when, sadly, he died. David Berry, who had joined British Land in 1970 and the Board in 1976, retired in 1998. He had been particularly active in building up the overseas business, notably in Australia. Stephen Kalman, who began at British Land in 1972, had primary responsibility for its development activity and served on the Board from 1989 to 1999 when he retired, though he remained

Michael Cassidy joined the Board in 1996 and is a practising solicitor.

Robert Swannell is Vice-Chairman of Citigroup Europe.

Bob Bowden came to British Land from Conrad Ritblat in 1992, having been at that firm with John Ritblat for 22 years.

Peter Simon, former
Deputy Chief Executive of
Legal & General Group.

Sir Derek Higgs became
Deputy Chairman of
British Land in 2001.

Lord Burns joined the
Board as a non-executive
director in 2000.

a consultant. Cyril Metliss, who joined the Company in January 1971 and became a director in July of that year, retired from the Board (though not from the Company itself) in 2003. In 2002 John Weston Smith became Chief Operating Officer and was succeeded as Finance Director by Graham Roberts, formerly a partner at Arthur Andersen.

There were changes in the non-executive directorate too. Michael Cassidy, a prominent City solicitor, who had served as chairman of the powerful Policy Committee of the Corporation of London, joined the Board in 1996 and John Spink retired in 1997. John Reynolds, Chairman of Corporate Finance for Europe at ABN Amro Bank, and previously at Schroders for 21 years, joined the Board in 1997. Unhappily he died at the early age of 50, only two years later. In 1999 Robert Swannell, then Vice-Chairman of Schroder Salomon Smith Barney, became a non-executive director. Peter Simon retired in 2000, having been a non-executive director since 1988 and serving as chairman of Board committees and as the senior independent non-executive director during his term of office. He remained as chairman of the Group Pension Scheme until 2005.

Derek (now Sir Derek) Higgs, formerly of S. G. Warburg and then an executive director of Prudential among other appointments, and Lord Burns, Permanent Secretary of H.M. Treasury 1991 – 1998 and a director then of Pearson and Legal & General Group, both joined the Board in 2000. Lord Burns left the Board in September 2005 on his appointment as Chairman-designate of Marks & Spencer. Sir Derek Higgs, who by then had achieved distinction through his eponymous report on corporate governance, left in July 2006 following his appointment as Chairman of Alliance & Leicester.

The senior executive at British Land was considerably expanded in the 1990s as the Group itself grew (and as business life became increasingly complicated). Tony Braine joined in 1987 and became

Nick Ritblat joined British Land in 1987 and became an executive director in 1991, leaving the Company in 2005. He is the current (2006) President of the British Property Federation.

Before joining the Board in 2006, Tim Roberts was Co-head of Asset Management.

All pulling together, or Three Men in a Boat – the Chairman takes the oars while Chief Operating Officer John Weston Smith relaxes in the bows and Finance Director Graham Roberts (newly arrived from Arthur Andersen and assisted here by Mr Moser) keeps a sharp lookout astern. The scene on the lake in Regent's Park has an almost pastoral simplicity and yet Regent's Place (overleaf) is barely a stone's throw away.

Company Secretary in 1995. Lucinda Bell joined in 1991, becoming Head of Tax in 2001 and then Head of Tax and Accounting in 2003. Peter Earl became Head of a small IT team in 1989, and remains Head of its much enlarged department. Sarah Barzycki joined in 1998 and covers a range of activities including banking and joint ventures. Adrian Penfold became Head of Planning in 1996 and later also Head of Environment. Nigel Webb became Head of Development in 2003, having joined the Company in 1992.

Two significant "Heads" outside Head Office are Barry Winfield, Managing Director of Broadgate Estates, which was acquired by British Land in 1996, and Mohammed Dajani, Managing Director of the Meadowhall Shopping Centre in Sheffield, which was acquired in 1999. Tim Roberts, who joined British Land in 1997 and has been a member of the Executive Committee since 2005, joined the Board as an Executive Director with responsibility for offices and other non-retail assets in July 2006. Peter Clarke, a former Assistant Secretary, also joined the Executive Committee in 2005, and has been appointed Executive Officer with a wide administrative and financing remit.

The strategy reiterated

The Company's office properties were now yielding handsome returns, and the expansion into retail was also bearing fruit. John Ritblat set out the Company's strategic thinking at length in his 2001 Statement.

‘We are in the business of buying and developing properties which will add to net asset value and thus total return. We finance this expenditure cheaply and limit our exposure to variable interest rates. We control debt to be roughly the same amount as our shareholders' funds, enabling us to deliver double any increase in value which the portfolio achieves, a particularly useful attribute in a time of low inflation.

Our policy remains to buy first class modern property in good locations, preferably with long leases to high quality tenants.

A profitable development programme is important to the Group. These developments often derive from investment purchases, Plantation Place, Regent's Place and East Kilbride being typical examples of replacing older properties or adding to existing investments.

In recent years we have used Joint Venturing to broaden our approach. Through joint ventures we secure properties off market, spread risk and procure additional financing with like-minded top quality partners. We earn fees as we are able to manage ventures to satisfy both our own and our partners' standards.

Our strategy is to anticipate financing needs. We raise funding when and where it is available rather than when it is required. Instantly accessible resources are essential to an active investor, for example in choosing the moment to redeem funding when it is advantageous – as with the Unsecured Bonds.

Our investment is always opportunistic – it is the nature of our business. Sellers are not waiting for us, nor is there a conveyor-belt of good properties on a predetermined basis. When, for instance, owners want to sell – provided that their properties qualify under our criteria – we will be buyers, and if the market is a bit queasy at the time, so much the better our bargaining position.

Opportunism is tempered by our aversion to risk, exemplified by:

• long leases with good covenants
• a diversified, largely freehold and modern portfolio
• long finance and low exposure to variable interest rates
• wariness in starting on major developments speculatively.

You are halfway to making money if you avoid losing any. 〕

He could, of course, have made much the same statement in 1971 – this effective strategy remained in place throughout John Ritblat's years at British Land.

The Euston Tower (far right) is one of the few remaining sections of the original Euston Centre, half of which was acquired by British Land in 1984 with the other half following in 1986. The development as a whole is now known as Regent's Place. In the centre of this view, looking north-east towards Hampstead Road with Euston station beyond, is the Abbey HQ, with Triton Square behind it. The tall white building, 338 Euston Road, was the first part of Regent's Place to be redeveloped. At the time of the photograph, construction of 350 Euston Road (bottom left) had reached the final stages – it is now complete and occupied. British Land's future plans for the site embrace expansion both northwards and westwards.

5

Into a New Era

Corporate raiders

Stephen Hester arrives

The pillars of Hercules

Sponsorship, sustainability and corporate responsibility

British Land in the community

Support for the arts, sports and education

Sir John Ritblat steps down

Transformation into a Real Estate Investment Trust

Two cast iron figures – one outside the building, one inside – study each other through the glass walls of 350 Euston Road. Anthony Gormley's *Reflection* (2001) shows how contemporary art has an integral role in British Land's developments.

'A pretty respectable inheritance...'

In 2002 the Company became the subject of the unwelcome attentions of a concern called Laxey Partners, resident in the Isle of Man. Using a ploy, Laxey Partners had acquired its interests in British Land through 105 subsidiaries each holding British Land shares, to propose three resolutions to be put to the 2002 Annual General Meeting. In reality, of course, there was only one requisitionist – Laxey. In brief, these resolutions sought British Land shareholder approval to compel the Board to undertake the mandatory repurchase of British Land shares by the Company, and to engage external property managers.

These controversial proposals achieved high levels of publicity, providing financial journalists with a hot topic through much of the first half of 2002. The *Financial Times* was particularly vocal, publishing no fewer than 38 pieces on the topic between late April and late July 2002, 13 of them in the week of the 2002 Annual General Meeting. Laxey succeeded in borrowing shares to build up an apparent 10% stake in British Land, taking advantage of the stock lending market which normally operates only to provide liquidity to institutional investors. British Land was able to refute the thinking behind the Laxey proposals and to expose at the actual Annual General Meeting the use of borrowed – institutional – stock. All the Laxey resolutions were defeated.

Though the Laxey incidents were an unwelcome distraction for the Board, they did not interrupt the pace of business activity in the Company. In 2001 BL Davidson, a joint venture with the Davidson family, had become the owner of Asda Property Holdings, which has a portfolio of retail warehouses and Central London offices. A package of 22 Homebase stores yielding 7% was bought for £156 million; the renowned Accenture Consulting pre-leased 375,000 sq ft at Plantation Place at a rent of £54 per sq ft. The next year saw the Company extend its Broadgate interests still further by buying 1 Appold Street and the unowned half of Broadgate Phase 12, which had created a raft over the railway lines from Liverpool Street Station. This is the site for the 35-storey Broadgate Tower and a further 13-storey building being developed (2006) at 201 Bishopsgate. Together the buildings provide over 820,000 sq ft of new office space.

David Michels, now Sir David, became a non-executive director in 2003.

Two new non-executive directors joined the Board at this time: Chris Gibson-Smith, Chairman of the London Stock Exchange and of National Air Traffic Services and formerly a group managing director of BP, and David Michels, then Chief Executive of Hilton Group. Dr Gibson-Smith was appointed senior independent non-executive director.

The Board's Nomination Committee then set out to select a new Chief Executive, and appointed Stephen Hester, aged 43, with effect from November 2004. At this point the roles of Chairman and Chief Executive were split, with John Ritblat remaining as Chairman. In contrast to the Chairman's 50-year stint in the property market, Stephen Hester's previous career had been in banking. He spent 20 years at Credit Suisse First Boston, rising through various appointments to become its Chief Financial Officer and Global Head of the Fixed Income Division in both New York and London. In May 2002 he joined Abbey National as its Chief Financial Officer, later being promoted to Chief Operating Officer. His leadership role there embraced strategy, risk, finance, financial markets and external communications. Coming from a non-property background, he has conducted a comprehensive review of the Company's structure and business and management. He has already introduced a number of changes, including the formation of an Executive Committee comprised of executive directors and other senior members of staff.

Stephen Hester brought to British Land a formidable intellect and great financial acumen. In November 2004 he became Chief Executive, with John Ritblat remaining as Chairman.

The first transaction Stephen Hester completed was a highly significant one – the acquisition of Pillar Property, which specialises in developing and investing in retail warehousing. This activity is carried out in conjunction with offshore fund managers, the funding being provided by independent investing institutions and individuals. Pillar had been set up by two successful entrepreneurs, Raymond Mould and Patrick Vaughan, who had previously run Arlington Securities, a developer of business parks. Pillar was formed in 1992 as a new venture between Arlington, Electra Investment Trust and the pension fund of The General Electric Company (USA). It was listed on the London Stock Exchange as a public company in July 1994 with a market value of £150 million.

Dr Chris Gibson-Smith became a non-executive director of British Land in January 2003 and was later appointed Deputy Chairman in 2006. He becomes Chairman in 2007. A distinguished career at BP, which he joined in 1970, culminated in his appointment as a Group Managing Director. He was a non-executive director of Lloyds TSB (1999–2005), Chairman of National Air Traffic Services Limited (2001–05), a director of Powergen (2001–02) and has been Chairman of the London Stock Exchange since 2003.

Initially Pillar was a general property investor but, over time, it restricted its interests to retail parks and the City of London. That was also the time when the process of focus made it clear that a wider ownership structure was appropriate. Higher-yielding and more targeted investment could best be achieved when Pillar permitted sellers of property to retain an interest. The Hercules Unit Trust began under the stewardship of Andrew Jones, seeded by a retail park portfolio from Equitable Life and by Fosse Park, a joint project between Pillar, Schroders, and la Caisse de Depot of Canada and by Pillar's direct retail park investments. At the start Pillar held a 49% stake in Hercules. It was also the start of the concept of a property company being both an investor in and the adviser to a pooled property vehicle.

Andrew Jones, elected to
the Board in 2006, had
been a director of Pillar.

Hercules was almost immediately followed by CLOUT, focussing on the City of London and seeded by capital from Schroders, Pillar and La Caisse de Depot and with property coming via a public bid for Wates City of London. 2004 saw the addition of the smaller park fund known as Hercules Income Fund. After two years of planning its entry into European retail parks, Pillar then embarked on a policy of investing abroad through its newest venture, the PREF fund. At the time of the deal that saw it become a key part of the British Land portfolio (July 2005), Pillar's assets under management exceeded £3 billion.

The way ahead

Sir John Ritblat chose the 2006 Annual General Meeting as the occasion at which he formally announced the decision that for so many years had seemed unthinkable.

'I have always spoken of property as a long-term business,' he told shareholders, 'and indeed I have been actively engaged in it for over half a century. I have told the Board that I would like to stand down at the end of 2006. The Company is in excellent shape after another record year and with management transition to Stephen Hester now successfully complete. I do not think it would be too immodest to say he has received a pretty respectable inheritance!

'I am proud and complimented that the Board has been kind enough to elect me Honorary President of the Company when I cease to be Chairman. My successor will be Dr Chris Gibson-Smith, who steps up to be our Deputy Chairman today, and in January he will be succeeded as Senior Independent Non-Executive Director by Sir David Michels.'

As the outgoing Chairman went on to remark, British Land had come a long way in a relatively short time. When he took over Union Property Holdings in 1969, it had assets of just £6 million and a share price measured in pennies. By 2006 the Company had assets owned and managed in excess of £18 billion and net assets per share of £15.

But a change of Chairman was not the only sign that a new era was emerging. As its 150th year of business drew to an end, British Land prepared to move into its new home, York House near Marble Arch. The building is a British Land development and so, for the first time in its long history, the Company will occupy a building it has itself created. More significantly, British Land is on the brink of being able to transform itself into an entirely new corporate form, a Real Estate Investment Trust (REIT). For some years British Land and particularly one of its directors, Nick Ritblat, was in the forefront of those pressing for REITs to be permitted in the United Kingdom. When the Government was eventually prepared to engage in discussions with the property industry, British Land's Head of Tax and Accounting, Lucinda Bell, represented the property companies in the intricate technical discussions which ensued.

Artist's impression of York House, British Land's new home near Marble Arch.

Lord Turnbull joined the Board as a non-executive director in 2006

Kate Swann was another non-executive appointment to the Board in 2006.

Patrick Vaughan, who retired in 2006, came to the Board from Pillar Property.

The effect will be to liberate British Land from liability to tax on capital gains and on profits for those activities within the REIT regime. A REIT is required to conform to various rules. The main one is an obligation to distribute 90% of its profits, and to ensure that rental income is at least $1\frac{1}{4}$ times the interest payment on debt. To enter the REIT regime, which has a start date of 1 January 2007, British Land will have to pay a one-off entry fee of 2% of its gross assets as a tax to the Government. The effect of this change is likely to make property held through a REIT more attractive to investors. Hitherto their holdings in property company shares have been depleted twice by the tax the company itself has paid, and then a second time by the tax the investors have themselves been obliged to pay on dividends and on capital gains on their shares. REITs give property companies a level playing field when competing for investors' funds.

Towards the next 150 years?

With a new Head Office, the new REIT business model, a new Chairman in Dr Chris Gibson-Smith and a recently appointed new Chief Executive in Stephen Hester, the Company has prepared itself well for the future. There have been other changes too. As already stated, Sir Derek Higgs retired from the Deputy Chairmanship and the Board in July 2006. At the same time two new non-executives joined the Board: Lord Turnbull, a former Secretary of the Cabinet and Head of the Home Civil Service, and Kate Swann, Chief Executive of W. H. Smith.

Meanwhile Patrick Vaughan, the former Chief Executive of Pillar, has retired, having helped the successful integration of that company as part of a wider contribution to British Land. John Weston Smith, who joined British Land in 1971 and served as Company Secretary, an executive director, head of British Land of America, Finance Director and finally Chief Operating Officer during his 35 years with the Company, also retired at the AGM in July 2006.

Two new executive directors were elected to the Board at the same time. Andrew Jones joined British Land with Pillar in 2005, after ten years with that company of which he was an executive director with responsibilities for retail park investment and asset management. At British Land he is co-head of asset management concentrating on the retail sector and retail funds. Tim Roberts joined British Land in 1997 and in 2002 became joint head of its asset management. He remains co-head of asset management, concentrating on the office sector of the Company's portfolio and with responsibility too for other significant elements.

In conclusion

Here this history of British Land necessarily ends, but happily it is in every sense unfinished business – and long may it remain so! There is every hope and expectation that it will – for, in an increasingly complex economy, property offers a reassuringly simple receptacle for savings and has a wide appeal for investors. What you see is what you get, and while it is tempting to think that little more than the name now connects the original British Land (née the National Freehold Land Society) with the 21st century, it would not be entirely true. From Moorgate Street to Marble Arch, from the forty-bob freehold to the Broadgate Estate, British Land has already spanned three centuries of Britain's history during which time its size, scope, modus operandi and economic framework have changed out of all recognition.

And yet there is a clear element of continuity as well, as this account has made plain: an awareness of the necessity of planning for the long-term side by side with the ability to capitalize on opportunities as they arise. As the largest British property company with a portfolio owned or managed of approaching £20 billion in 2006, British Land has successfully adapted to changing needs over its long history. It has the stability, the financial muscle and the entrepreneurial energy to surpass its previous achievements, serving well the communities that use its buildings and the pension funds and other investors who rely on it for capital and dividend growth.

Beyond History – Doing Something for Others

Warehouse? Inspired by British Land's broadsheets on form and function in building design, children seized on the practical possibilities of property development. One aspiring young architect from a West London primary school even made the cover of the Company's 1994 Annual Report.

'As the Company has grown, so has the extent of its impacts on others and its ability to respond to their needs...'

British Land has sponsored many performances by the National Youth Orcherstra.

Outside and beyond its own 150 year history, an entirely different (and sometimes unsuspected) dimension to British Land has been its awareness of its obligation in and to the community. Nowadays these obligations have the grand title of corporate responsibility, and have to refer to stakeholders, which really means all the various groups and individuals who are affected by what the Company does – or doesn't – do.

As the Company has grown, so has the extent of its impacts on others and its ability to respond to their needs. Since 2003 British Land has issued Corporate Responsibility Reports which record in some considerable detail the Company's progress on topics such as managing waste disposal effectively and reducing carbon emissions and energy and water use. For new buildings British Land has devised its own Sustainability Brief, which guides the entire development process. This applies to environmental and community impacts before development starts, through design and construction, to user and occupier satisfaction and continuing dialogue afterwards.

Here are just a few of the many activities in which British Land and its staff have been engaged in recent years:

• Teams from Head Office – including newly integrated Pillar employees – and Broadgate Estates were involved in volunteering initiatives at Abney Park Cemetery and City Farm in the Borough of Hackney. The two projects were selected from a list compiled by the East London Business Alliance (ELBA) and aligned with British Land's desire to work on activities that contribute directly to the environment and communities of Hackney, close to Broadgate, the Company's major City of London investment. Abney Park Cemetery is a heritage site and wildlife habitat visited annually by some 6,000 schoolchildren from inner city areas. A team of 40 volunteers cleared overgrown woodland and prepared ground for wildflower planting. Hackney City Farm helps inner city children to understand the origins of the food they eat, and also provides a first rung on the employment ladder for young school leavers and the long-term unemployed. Over two tough but rewarding days, 40 volunteers undertook gardening, land clearance and basic building on the farm.

• The Meadowhall Action Team – consisting of employees from many of the Centre's operating areas – helped to redecorate the local Community Resource Centre at Darnall, on the east side of Sheffield. Cleaning, clearing and decorating gave the Community Resource Centre a much needed new look.

• At Canada Water, a new mixed office and residential development with community facilities in London's Docklands, the British Land Canada Quays joint venture partnership has worked closely with the local authority and land owner, the London Borough of Southwark, to undertake a comprehensive, long-term consultation programme in the neighbouring communities. Members of these communities with a stake in the future of Canada Water are helping to guide and shape the regeneration Masterplan for the area. In 2005, two phases of community consultation took place. The first focused on interviews and workshops with a targeted group of stakeholders and opinion formers. The second involved a series of workshops open to members of the wider community.

Many local interest groups were engaged in Phase One, including the Canada Water Consultation Forum, ward councillors, the Canada Water Campaign Group, the Rotherhithe Area Housing Forum and the Southwark Disability Forum. British Land advertised the consultation programme through a newsletter to local households and notices in the local press. The Company also provided additional services, including free shuttle buses, a care allowance scheme for parents and carers attending the event, and consultation materials in a variety of formats and languages. Each phase of consultation was conducted with advice from Southwark Council officers and staffed by core members of the British Land Canada Quays team.

The arrival at Cornwall Terrace of another doorstep-sized volume on corporate and social responsibility is greeted by scenes of wild elation. Drawing by Gerard Hoffnung, from the 2004 Annual Report.

A total of 78 people attended the two phases of consultation, and an additional 400 attended a subsequent Masterplan exhibition held at The Event at Southwark Park in July, where they could see the development plans on display panels and as 3-D models. 161 attendees completed feedback forms, with 75% supportive of the Masterplan's proposals. Planning Permission was granted for the proposals in October 2006.

• British Land staff, working through the Education Business Partnership in Camden, London NW1, provide reading support to children at Netley Primary School. 20 employees are taking part in the scheme, with teams of readers visiting the school every week. This activity dovetails with the Company's commitment to reading being a fundamental skill for all children. Volunteers reported being particularly motivated by seeing their reading partners developing socially and academically.

• British Land staff also participate in Partnerships in Leadership, matching business partners to head teachers.

In addition to community-based ventures, British Land undertakes wider sponsorships with the objective of investing in the future through education, the arts and sport. In the early 1990s the Company, in conjunction with the Design Council, produced an award-winning series of Educational Broadsheets which were distributed to schools throughout the United Kingdom. Among the themes covered were the evolution of shops and housing, buildings for education and the architecture of public transport. The common feature was the property element, for so many human activities rely on buildings which, whether we are aware of it or not, play a major role in shaping the fabric of our everyday lives as well as defining the environment in which we live. These broadsheets were very successful in helping children understand the connection between a building's form and its practical function.

The Company is a major sponsor of the National Literacy Trusts's Initiative 'Reading is Fundamental'

One of the award-winning series of broadsheets which were distributed to a total of 30,000 schools throughout the United Kingdom. Developed by British Land in partnership with CDT Design and the Design Council. Their themes and content were closely linked to the requirements of the National Curriculum.

Overleaf – The staff and pupils of Thomas Jones Primary School make good use of the Company's educational broadsheets. In other London schools, British Land volunteers help with reading support.

houses

Turf hut ...

Anglo-Saxon house ...

Thatched cottage ...

Manor house ...

Timber-framed house ...

Long house ...

Buildings have as much character as a human face, and few are more expressive than the houses on this broadsheet from The British Land Company PLC.

Houses rarely retain the exact form in which they were built, for with time their owners' requirements subtly change. And yet, as these examples show, there is often a strong sense of continuity and tradition evident in the design of buildings.

Studied carefully, they reveal stories that are rich in insights — into the age in which these houses were built, into the people who lived in them and the use they made of their homes, as well as changes in architectural fashions, construction and craftsmanship over the years.

Brick-built house ...

Georgian town house ...

Weaver's cottage ...

Industrialist's mansion ...

Factory workers' terraces ...

Suburban semi ...

International style ...

Prefabricated bungalow ...

High-rise flats ...

Modern estate housing ...

Energy-efficient home ...

Numbers refer to a series published by The British Land Company PLC. The text written by The British Land Design has been an active and highly respected developer of business properties. It has a long-term commitment to preserving and conserving the architectural heritage of Britain.

Tension mounts at the 2000 British Land UK Chess Challenge, held at Alexandra Palace. Of close to 40,000 entrants that year, just 930 made it through to the Gigafinals. The youngest competitor was five years old.

(RIF), which provides thousands of children with motivational activities, opportunities for family and community involvement, and up to three free books each year to choose and keep, together with a book bag, bookmark, bookplates and stickers. On World Book Day in March 2005, seven schools in the Woking area (totalling 500 children) joined the RIF project. The Woking scheme brings together a number of partners including the SHINE partnership, the Surrey Library Service and British Land's Peacocks Shopping Centre. In September 2005, 16 primary schools in the Sheffield area (in all some 900 children) joined the scheme, with the help of partners including Sheffield Libraries Service, Family with Learning and Meadowhall Shopping Centre. A further 12 primary schools in Camden joined the same month, supported by partners including the Camden Local Education Authority and library service and British Land's Head Office. The RIF initiative also gives children the chance to hear stories and meet authors and illustrators. The programme aims to fire the imagination of children and foster their long-term love of reading.

For some years now the British Land UK Chess Challenge has attracted entries from thousands of schools and tens of thousands of competitors. As well as arranging direct publicity for the Challenge, British Land featured it on the cover of its 2000 Interim Report. This brought the competition to the notice of the wider, non-educational audience of shareholders and the other stakeholders with interests in British Land.

The London Business School has been supported both financially and practically, by regular gifts of money and by John Ritblat's membership of its Governing body, providing his specialist advice on its property affairs. Having been Deputy Chairman, in 2006 he was appointed its Chairman.

It is almost impossible for art galleries with constrained budgets to meet the considerable expense of assembling and putting on special exhibitions. British Land was the sole sponsor of Wright of Derby at the Tate (1990) which went on to the Grand Palais in

Paris and then the Metropolitan Museum in New York. His two most celebrated paintings, "A Philosopher Lecturing on the Orrery" (1776) and "An Experiment on a Bird in the Air Pump" (1768) representing a complex synthesis of art, science and philosophy were both included in a wide-ranging show. Three years later, again at the Tate, the Company was sole sponsor of the Ben Nicholson Centenary Exhibition, covering the various phases of his development as an artist during his long life.

Thomas Gainsborough has been the subject of two British Land sponsorships, The Young Gainsborough at the National Gallery in 1996, and a major exhibition of his work at Tate Britain in 2002. His enormous – yet intimate – portraits are almost overpowering in their intensity when seen assembled together, especially if seen in an empty gallery before visitors arrive.

In the autumn of 2004 the Company sponsored an exhibition of the luscious work of François Boucher at a new venue, the Wallace Collection, only a few yards from the site of Conrad Ritblat's original offices. This was entitled, appropriately enough, Seductive Visions and featured balmy pastorals, large numbers of ladies and a notable portrait of the artist's celebrated patron, Madame de Pompadour.

To greet the start of British Land's 150th year it sponsored an exhibition at Tate Britain entitled Degas, Sickert and Toulouse-Lautrec, London and Paris 1870 –1910, which later moved on to The Phillips Collection in Washington DC. The primary linking theme was Degas and his friendships with British artists and French artists working in Britain: some of these artists were also represented in the exhibition.

2006 saw British Land's important sponsorship of 'Holbein in England' at Tate Britain. This was the first major UK exhibition devoted to Hans Holbein the Younger for more than half a century and included many iconic portraits alongside their preparatory sketches giving a fascinating insight into Holbein's working methods and showed the great beauty of his work.

Gainsborough's 1771 portrait of Edward, Viscount Ligonier, from the 2002 Interim Report. That year British Land sponsored a major exhibition of the artist's work at Tate Britain.

Ballet, too, has been the subject of British Land sponsorships – Le Tricorne at the Royal Opera House in 1995, and Romeo and Juliet in 2001. The Company supported the Royal Ballet School for its move to new premises in Covent Garden, as well as the Royal Opera House's renovation and expansion in 1997. Nor is music neglected – the Royal Academy of Music, the London Symphony Orchestra and the Monteverdi Choir are among a host of beneficiaries of British Land's enthusiastic support. At the less grand end, Paint Your Wagon at the Regent's Park Open Air Theatre was a particular favourite.

Then there is sport. The British Ski Championships became The British Land British Ski Championships in 1978 and are now in their 28th year of sponsorship. British Land also provides funding for our Olympic ski team. The game of Real Tennis, the precursor of Lawn Tennis, is a sport that at different times has been played with great enthusiasm and no little skill by both Henry VIII and John Ritblat (not together, of course). It has been enjoying a revival in recent years and British Land has aided its recovery by sponsoring the British Real Tennis Championships since 1994. The Company has also supported the leading professional squash rackets tournament played in a specially erected court in the Broadgate Circle.

Other examples from a long list of ways in which the Company lends a hand are: providing bicycles for police at Regent's Park, and funding for the Royal Parks at the Museum of London, Sadlers Wells Theatre and Capital Cricket, a competition for London's young cricketers. The Company is always closely involved in the organisations and events it sponsors: it is not merely a chequebook supporter. As a case in point Tony Braine, the Company Secretary, who joined British Land in 1987, takes responsibility for the Schools Chess Championship, while Peter Clarke, Executive Officer, who joined the Company's Secretariat in 1989, is also Deputy Chairman of the British Ski and Snowboard Federation.

The Royal Ballet School, one of the world's great academies of talent.

It's downhill all the way from now on…

Real Tennis (right) – 'the King of Games, the Game of Kings…'.

More than just a statutory document...

For the past two decades British Land has used its Annual Report and Accounts as both a formal record of its business activities and as a way of highlighting to shareholders the strength of its corporate culture. This has been done in imaginative and at times unexpected ways that celebrate the special relationship the Company enjoys with the organisations it supports in the field of education, the arts and sport. Initiated by Sir John Ritblat and created by CDT Design with his knowledgeable input, the quality of these Annual Reports has been recognised by a stream of awards.

1991 Tate Gallery:
British landscape painting

1992 National Museum of Photography,
Film & Television: Landscape photography

1993 Ben Nicholson at the Tate

1994 Educational broadsheets

1995 Corn Exchange murals

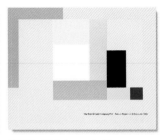

1996 Community sponsorship

1997 The National Gallery

1998 Real Tennis: British Land British
Open & Amateur Championships

1999 Royal Academy of Music

2000 London Zoo

2001 Museum of London

2002 Royal Ballet School

2003 London's Royal Parks

2004 British book illustrators

2005 Heritage and conservation

2006 National Portrait Gallery:
Born in 1856

The accompanying document:
British Life in the 1850's

British Land:
A Chronology
1970–2006

The ups and downs of the
property game – illustration
by William Heath Robinson
from the 2004 Annual
Report. British Land is an
enthusiastic sponsor of
Capital Kids Cricket, which
encourages young people's
interest in the sport.

1970

Conrad Ritblat & Co and various private property company interests controlled by the Conrad and Ritblat families acquired by Union Property Holdings (London). John Ritblat joins Union's board as Managing Director.

British Land the subject of reverse takeover bid from Union Properties. John Ritblat becomes Managing Director of British Land.

Net Assets at 31 March 1970	£15m

1971

British Land acquires Regis Property Holdings, which owns a number of properties in the West End and City of London, including Plantation House.

John Ritblat appointed Executive Chairman.

Net Assets at 31 March 1971	£26m

1972

Classic Cinema Chain (part of the original Union portfolio) sold for £7m.

Agreement reached with House of Fraser to acquire the former Derry & Toms department store jointly with clothing retailer Dorothy Perkins.

A £10m 8.5% revolving credit facility arranged with Mercantile Credit which subscribes for 1.5m British Land shares at 135p per share.

Acquisition of 73.5% of W. Crowther & Sons, a publicly quoted brick manufacturer.

The Croydon Centre (382,500 sq ft offices and 215,000 sq ft retail) acquired for £9.7m.

Net Assets at 31 March 1972	£48m

1973

Three joint office development schemes with a potential investment value of £40–50m (Caxton House, Romney House and Avenue des Arts, Brussels) announced with Commercial Union.

A 135,000 sq ft office and retail investment at 56 Rue Du Faubourg St. Honoré and 4–14 Rue D'Agusseau, Paris acquired for £5m.

A 26% interest acquired in Dominion Properties Pty, a quoted Australian company.

Agreement reached to acquire 110–122 Aldersgate St, EC1 at a cost of £4.25m.

Kingsway Hall, Carlton House, Wesley House and International Buildings, Holborn acquired for around £2.5m.

£10m 5-year loan provided by the Crown Agents at 8.25%.

British Land's unsecured Euro dollar borrowing raises $16m at 8% repayable in 1987.

British Land bids £2m for Hardun Bux (which, in addition to various non-property interests, owns development sites at West Drayton and near Norwich).

Joint company formed with Turriff to develop surplus land owned by the North Thames Gas Board.

C.E. Coates, a Section 123 bank, becomes a British Land subsidiary.

Net Assets at 31 March 1973	£127.5m

1974

Agreed tender offer announced for Uris Buildings Corporation of New York, valuing that company at US$153m. Offer reduced to US$127m following reassessment of Uris's net asset value, and rejected in the face of a higher counter-offer from National Kinney Corporation.

Agreed offer for Dorothy Perkins, which also has a 75% interest in Biba.

A 15 acre trading estate in Bilston acquired for a little over £1m.

Planning consent agreed in principle for the development of 150,000 sq.ft offices and 60,000 sq ft shops at Clapham Junction.

Rent freeze and first letting tax imposed; MLR raised to "crisis" level of 13%.

The Group resumes its expansion overseas with the acquisition of three properties in California.

A portfolio of investment properties in Holland acquired at a cost of around £25m.

Net Assets at 31 March 1974	£126m

1975

British Land sells its 26% stake in Dominion Properties (the Group's plans for the company having been frustrated by Australian government policies).

The Company makes the first property sale of its degearing programme – a development in Harrow, with vacant possession.

Net Assets at 31 March 1975	£110m

1976

A 144,000 sq ft office building in Brisbane acquired and leased back for six years to the vendor who in turn sub-lets to the Australian government.

Biba to be closed and Marks & Spencer to move into part of the Kensington store.

89,000 sq ft offices in Bourke Street, Melbourne sold to the Australian government.

Net Assets at 31 March 1976	£98m

1977

A 50% interest in the Group's Dutch subsidiary sold to Wereldhave.

BHS agree to lease 120,000 sq ft of the former Derry & Toms/Biba building in Kensington High Street.

C.E. Coates (the Group's Section 123 banking subsidiary) sold to United City Merchants.

Part of the Croydon Centre sold to Legal & General's pensions management fund.

The balance of the equity of W. Crowther not already owned acquired for £1.1m.

The entire 20,000 sq ft refurbishment of 8 Lloyds Avenue EC3 fully let to four tenants.

Further properties in the Croydon Centre sold to the Gas Staff Pension Fund.

Legal & General acquires the commercial element of Fizhardinge House, Portman Square for £1.5m (the residential element having been sold on a long ground lease in 1973).

25–25a Church St and 8–12 Williamson St, Liverpool sold.

Net Assets at 31 March 1977	£47m

1978

Tai Cheung Properties (an affiliate of Hutchinson International) discloses a 10.02% stake in British Land.

A 15.5% stake in Bridgewater Estates acquired from Rothschild Investment Trust in exchange for 2.07m British Land shares.

A 50% interest in British Land's French subsidiary owning 56 Rue du Faubourg St Honoré and 4–14 Rue D'Aguesseau Paris is sold to Wereldhave.

Major refinancing, successfully concluded, places the company's finances on a sound footing.

£1.1m received from the sale of the Group's 15.5% stake in Bridgewater Estates.

British Land's interest in the 250,000 sq ft Setanta office development in Dublin sold for £12m.

British Land moves its headquarters from 35/38 Portman Square to Cornwall Terrace, Regent's Park (re-letting its former space to Marathon Oil and gaining an immediate net revenue benefit of around £0.2m p.a).

An 11.5% interest in Property Investment & Finance (PIF) acquired in exchange for 1.05m British Land shares.

British Land's stake in PIF increased to 18.3% resulting in the issue of a further 780,000 British Land shares.

A 100,000 sq.ft office building in Lille sold for around £3m.

The sale of the 400,000 sq.ft Liverpool Exchange office building raises £38.6m.

British Land's 18.8% stake in PIF sold for £0.73m.

Fire damages some 70,000 sq ft of Plantation House: fully insured.

Net Assets at 31 March 1978   £49m

1979

The newly developed 120 Aldersgate Street (29,000 sq ft) let to the Post Office for around £0.3m p.a.

1.9m British Land shares issued to acquire a 15.6% stake in Churchbury Estates.

CQC, a specialist clothing manufacturer for the defence and other industries, acquired for £1.2m cash.

800 Wilshire Boulevard, Los Angeles sold realising US$4.5m.

Kingsmere Investment Company acquired for £4.2m (comprising 5.44m British Land shares plus £1m cash on completion and £1.35m in cash or shares a year after completion).

6.8m British Land shares plus £1.5m cash issued to acquire a 26.22% stake in the City Offices Company. Stake then increased to 29%.

A 96,800 sq ft office development "Les Tres Fontaines" at Cergy Pontoise sold for £3m.

A pre-tax profit of £0.26m announced for the half year to September 1978 – British Land's first pre-tax profit for more than five years.

British Land's 29% stake in City Offices sold to Legal & General for £6.6m.

British Land's 20.3% stake in Churchbury Estates sold to London Trust for £1.2m.

Net Assets at 31 March 1979   £81m

1980

The Langham Estate (acquired in September 1978 on the acquisition of Kingsmere Estates) sold for £9m (a profit of £4.8m).

£11.1m raised from the sale of the leasehold shopping interests in the former Derry & Toms store.

Canning House, Edinburgh sold for £2.7m.

The Group's investment properties in Australia to be transferred to Postland Property Trust (to be owned jointly with the Post Office Superannuation Fund and Conzinc Riotinto Staff Provident Fund) in exchange for a 24.5% stake in the new entity and A$19m in cash.

Dorothy Perkins sold to Burton Group in a complex deal involving a consideration of around £21m (£4.6m in cash and £10.5m represented by the transfer of 74 Burton Group Investment Properties to British Land. British Land also retained a £3.3m dividend from

Dorothy Perkins while Burton assumed responsibility for an outstanding debt of £2.5m).

Net Assets at 31 March 1980	£119m

1981

20 Soho Square W1 (65,000 sq ft offices) sold for £0.75m.

British Land pays £11.1m for the Corn Exchange Company and £21m for the United Kingdom Property Company (satisfied by the issue of 24.97m ordinary shares).

The Group announces a holding of 4.9% in J Hepworth & Son.

A portfolio of five retail properties sold to National Freight Pension Fund for just over £3m.

The 145 acre Denham site sold for £8.35m.

Jarvis Brothers & Brewster (Construction), a Worthing-based housebuilder, acquired for £1.82m (met from the issue of 0.49m shares and £0.5m in cash).

Net Assets at 31 March 1981	£168m

1982

British Land announces the negotiation of a "Drop-Lock" loan facility giving it the right to raise at least £30m at fixed rates of interest until August 1991.

Net Assets at 31 March 1982	£189m

1983

British Land acquires a 31% equity stake in Growth Realty Companies of California plus an unsecured loan stock with conversion rights and warrants attached (which, if exercised, would increase its interest in the company to 73%) at a cost of US$12.34m.

British Land discloses having built up a 5.61% stake in Manders Holdings, which is subsequently sold.

90 Broad Street, New York, USA (320,000 sq.ft of offices) acquired at a cost of some US$30m. The equity holding in Growth Realty increased to 35.9%.

The Group's leasehold interests in various properties – most notably 88/90 Regent Street W1 and 99/121 Kensington High Street W8 – are the subject of a rearrangement whereby in consideration for a total cost of £7m the leases are extended to 99 years on a nominal rental basis without rent review.

Net Assets at 31 March 1983	£205m

1984

Growth Realty enters into a US$41m joint venture to reconstruct "The Sofia", a 24 storey office/residential building in Manhattan.

A joint company – Comfort Lodge – formed with Comfort Hotels to build a small chain of hotels. Each parent company to provide £1m of equity and British Land a further £8m in the form of partly convertible 5 year loan capital.

A new joint venture company, Guildhall Investment Management, formed with Brian Banks as part of British Land's plans to expand its interests in the provision of financial services.

A joint venture company is formed with an Irish company, Power Securities, to develop 28,500 sq ft offices at 88/91 St Stephen's Green, Dublin.

Growth Realty changes its name to British Land of America.

A portfolio of 9 properties sold to Dares Estates, financed by a £2.5m loan from British Land and £1.85m in cash, of which £1m is used to subscribe for new shares (equivalent to 15% of Dares' enlarged equity) at 17.5p per share.

A 3.2% holding in Stock Conversion acquired from George Wimpey, then subsequently placed in the market.

A 50% interest in Euston Centre Properties acquired from Wimpey Property Holdings for £31.5m.

British Land International arranged to borrow some £40m by means of an issue of a 6.75% 12 year Swiss Franc Bonds with effect from 8 March 1984.

Jointly with Power Securities, British Land pays £5m to acquire a second site at St Stephen's Green, Dublin for a retail and office scheme.

Central Savings Bank Building, (formerly known as the Arlington Federal Building) Baltimore, Maryland, USA sold for US$24m.

Net Assets at 31 March 1984   £237m

1985

Two UK industrial properties, Avon House, 275/287 Borough High Street SE1 and Britannia House 15/23 Trinity Street SE1 sold for £1.5m.

The Cowley Centre, Oxford acquired for £4.3m.

A portfolio of five properties sold to Berkeley & Hay Hill Investments for £2.15m.

The Group's 24.5% interest in Postland Property Trust sold for over A$15.25m.

An agreed £11m bid by British Land for Gripperrods (manufacturers and suppliers of carpet laying equipment and accessories) will more than double the size of the Group's industrial division in terms of both profits and capital employed.

The Group announces the acquisition of 315 Park Avenue South, New York, USA, a 280,000 sq ft net office building for around US$33m.

New 6.5% 15 year Swiss Franc Bonds issued to raise £25m.

Agreement reached with Stockley and Barclays Bank Pension Fund to fund a major refurbishment

with Unilever of their head office complex in Salisbury Square, London EC4 at a cost of £13m.

Net Assets at 31 March 1985   £243m

1986

Planning consent granted for a total of 550,000 sq ft at Plantation House.

Equitable Debenture and Assets Corporation acquired for £19.15m, with a further payment of £1.35m when certain works are completed. Equitable's portfolio includes shopping centres at Cheltenham, Doncaster and Plymstock.

The Paternoster Consortium, in which British Land has a 20% stake, acquires 4.5 acres adjacent to St Paul's Cathedral.

The remaining Australian property in Perth is sold for A$6.5m.

Dutch Government agrees to lease the 500,000 sq ft office complex in Rijswijk jointly owned with Wereldhave.

Gripperrods' South African subsidiary sold.

Net Assets at 31 March 1986   £280m

1987

The purchase of 40 properties from Legal & General Assurance (Pensions Management) for £93m completed.

Profitable sales of property and other interests realise £87m.

The purchase of the freehold office buildings at 53 Eastcheap and 36/42 Fenchurch Street, London EC3 for £37m increases the site area of the Plantation House complex to 2.1 acres.

The £60m Brunel Centre development in London Docklands, in which British Land had a one-third interest, is under construction for completion early in 1989. Included are 250,000 sq ft of offices, a 240-room hotel and 120 residential units which are already pre-committed to international operators.

The £55m office building at 56 Rue du Faubourg, St Honoré, Paris (50% interest) is completely refurbished and re-let at three times previous rents.

The integration of 90 Broad Street into British Land of America Inc. is concluded, creating an entity listed on the New York Stock Exchange, with net assets of £47m.

The mature industrial subsidiaries Crowther Brickmakers, Bux Group, CQC, Westberga Industri AB and Beclawat are sold for a total consideration of £23.7m compared with a book value of £15.8m. The major industrial subsidiary still owned by the Group is Gripperrods International.

£50m bank multi option unsecured loan facility arranged with a five year term.

Share placing to finance in part the purchase of the Euston Centre.

Net Assets at 31 March 1987	£493m

1988

The sale of properties realise £160m.

The Gripperrods manufacturing business is sold.

Cereal House next to the Corn Exchange is first mooted as a development site.

British Land selected as joint developer on the Custom House Dock site, Dublin.

A £150m 9 year unsecured loan facility arranged.

British Land purchases the outstanding 85.2% of "B" ordinary shares in Rosehaugh Greycoat Estates (RGE) to be satisfied by issuing £18.7m worth of new British Land shares at 261p. The "B" shares converted into 29% of RGE. The only asset in this company is a 29.9% interest in

1 Finsbury Avenue EC2 (250,000 sq ft).

British Land acquires a £97m portfolio of primarily industrial property from 3i.

A planning application is submitted to redevelop Plantation House to provide 840,000 sq ft.

Plans formulated to build an additional 290,000 sq ft of space at the Euston Centre, now re-named Regent's Place.

The 20% holding in the Paternoster complex sold to Mountleigh.

Equity interest in British Land of America is reorganised.

Net Assets at 31 March 1988	£791m

1989

17 Sainsbury supermarkets purchased on sale and leasebacks.

Rise in London office values increases the City office portfolio to around 45% of gross assets.

British Land's stake in Control Securities is sold for some £40m.

Private placement arranged of £115m 10.77% fixed interest unsecured long-term bonds.

Net Assets at 31 March 1989	£1,033m

1990

Further five-year evergreen unsecured loan facility for £250m put in place.

Proposals put forward to de-merge the Group into New British Land and Old British Land but are withdrawn on 18 December 1989.

Between March 1989 and September 1990 around £270m is spent on acquisitions, including £81m for J Sainsbury Supermarkets; £95m for Gateway (now Somerfield) sale and leasebacks; Chesterfield House, adjoining Plantation House;

four office buildings totalling 257,000 sq ft on a yield of 9.25%.

| Net Assets at 31 March 1990 | £963m |

1991

Between January 1989 and June 1990 net debt has risen by £230m on the back of a stated acquisition strategy.

A £175m five-year unsecured revolving credit facility is arranged.

At March 1991 gearing reaches 85% with around half of the debt at variable rates. Some 40% of the rent roll is subject to guaranteed uplifts.

Some 15 further supermarkets are acquired from J Sainsbury for £135m. The lease term is 35 years and the initial yield 9.25%. The minimum annual uplifts are 7% in years 0–5 and 6% in years 6–10. The consideration is satisfied by £36.25m in cash, and £78.75m worth of Convertible Capital Bonds which converted into Ordinary shares at a 19% premium to the then share price.

| Net Assets at 31 March 1991 | £907m |

1992

Purchase of the entire outstanding freehold interests in 1, 2 and 3 Finsbury Avenue.

A 128,000 sq ft office building in Reading is acquired funded by cash and 3.5m shares at 303p.

A 24.4% stake in Five Oaks is bought for around £3m satisfied by the issue of British Land Ordinary shares to the vendor. Investments are also made in companies Chelsfield and Moorfields.

British Land states that property additions since the end of 1989 exceed £460m.

| Net Assets at 31 March 1992 | £804m |

1993

The retail warehouse interest is expanded with additions at Stockton (£22m) and Chester (£13m). Total purchases amount to £166m.

£115m Convertible Capital Bonds 2011 converted to Cumulative Convertible Redeemable Preference Shares.

Total ownership of 258,000 sq ft Atrium Twin Towers in Amsterdam achieved.

Next phase of the International Financial Services Centre at Dublin planned.

| Net Assets at 31 March 1993 | £775m |

1994

British Land issues £200m worth of First Mortgage Debenture Stock 2028. The effective coupon was 9.375%, equivalent to 90bp above the comparable long dated gilt. The Group introduced a new substitution clause to the debenture market which has subsequently been widely adopted.

4 for 17 rights issue at 245p to raise £132m in order to set up a joint fund with the Quantum Fund. Quantum subscribes for 11.3m shares at 298p.

British Land confirms that it has first right of refusal over Quantum's 50% investment in the joint venture and that after 2002 British Land has the right to buy out the other shareholders at the previous valuation. So far the joint venture has purchased £135m of property out of a planned £1bn.

Issue of £150m 8.875% unsecured bonds due 2023.

A 29.9% equity stake in Stanhope (owner of 50% of the Broadgate complex in the City of London) is acquired from the Bank of Nova Scotia.

British Land raises £150m through the issue of irredeemable convertible bonds. The coupon is 6% and the conversion price into ordinary shares 510p, some 25% above the then share price.

Net Assets at 31 March 1994 £1,307m

1995

British Land acquires the outstanding 51.5% of the joint venture with Quantum for £142m. The joint venture had gross property assets of £588m, which were valued on a 7.2% running yield.

British Land makes an agreed offer for the share capital of Stanhope of 3p per share and purchases Stanhope's bank debt of £122m.

Placing and open offer on the basis of 1 for 5 new ordinary shares to raise £210.7m. The proceeds are used to finance the acquisition of Stanhope which cost £135.1m.

Net Assets at 31 March 1995 £1,579m

1996

Issue of £250m 8.875% First Mortgage Debenture Bonds 2035. The effective coupon after pricing is 8.77%.

Some £222.5m is raised through a 1 for 6 placing and open offer to fund a portfolio of seven Tesco stores and three retail warehouse parks.

Agreement is reached with the Receiver of Rosehaugh to purchase the outstanding 50% interest in Broadgate Properties, for £120m. The transaction is completed in January 1996.

A mixed portfolio of 19 properties, mainly supermarkets, are sold to Daejan for £82.5m (9% initial yield). Further sales made since March 1995 include Summit House EC2 (£30m).

Joint venture formed with Scottish & Newcastle, to be known as The Public House Company.

Net Assets at 31 March 1996 · £1,869m

1997

Announcement that a planning application is to be submitted to the City Corporation for the development of 1m sq ft at Plantation House, to be named Plantation Place.

British Land completes a £114m securitisation of 135 Bishopsgate, acquired as part of Broadgate Properties. The financing is secured for 22 years on the rental stream from NatWest Markets, which occupies the building. The coupon is fixed at 8.47%.

£93m worth of Tesco supermarkets are sold into a joint venture with Tesco, which also sell £82m worth of property under sale and leaseback arrangements. Each party subscribes for £17.5m of equity and the rest of the consideration is debt.

The Group announces a joint venture with GUS, called BL Universal, which purchases £900m worth of principally retail property from GUS. The joint venture is to be financed through bank debt, shareholder loans and equity.

Net Assets at 31 March 1997 £2,337m

1998

Completion (two months early) of Phase One of Regent's Place, a 220,000 sq.ft building which is 70% pre-let to First National Bank of Chicago.

British Land issues £300m Convertible Bonds due 2007 at an interest rate of 6.5%.

Mixed portfolio of properties sold to Alony Hetz for £140m.

New 50:50 joint venture company with Rank Group created to acquire over £100m of leisure properties from Rank by way of purchase and leaseback.

British Land buys 100 Liverpool Street (382,000 sq ft) at Broadgate as a purchase and leaseback to a UBS subsidiary for £240m.

155 Bishopsgate, a Broadgate building of 410,000 sq ft, acquired for £203m.

New £420m joint venture partnership formed with Tesco to acquire £330m of properties, predominantly let to Tesco, from British Land and Tesco, and incur £90m of development expenditure.

Net Assets at 31 March 1998	**£2,932m**

1999

British Land enters into a further joint venture by buying a 50% interest in the 325,000 sq ft Peacocks Centre in Woking. Its partner is the Centre's developer SPP Investment Management.

Ground rents in five office buildings at Broadgate acquired from Railtrack for £140m.

Long leasehold of 175 Bishopsgate (385,000 sq ft) at Broadgate acquired for £206m.

British Land and Railtrack form joint venture to develop the next phase of Broadgate.

The Broadgate Club health club business sold to Holmes Place for £6.7m.

Planning consent for 1m sq ft of offices secured at Plantation Place.

Option entered into to acquire Meadowhall Shopping Centre near Sheffield for £1.17bn.

BL Universal buys the Beehive Centre, a retail park at Cambridge, and the Microsoft Campus, three buildings totalling 238,100 sq ft let to Microsoft at Thames Valley Park, Reading.

Mixed portfolio of nine properties sold to an overseas investor for £260m.

Net Assets at 31 March 1999	**£3,118m**

2000

£1.54bn issue of securised debt supported by cash flows from Broadgate completed.

Joint venture agreed with Dunloe Ewart to develop a 365 acre site at Cherrywood, Loughlinstown, Co Dublin.

£200m sale of City of London and other London properties announced, including the Corn Exchange.

Minority interest in the Swiss Centre, Leicester Square acquired for £10m.

Pre-letting agreed with Abbey National for new 196,000 sq ft headquarters at Regent's Place.

New joint venture arranged with House of Fraser to acquire BL Fraser for £173m and leaseback 15 department stores.

Purchase of Hamilton House (88,000 sq ft.) and Broadgate House and Eldon House.

Sale of 92 BLU properties to finance the purchase of retail parks in Cambridge, Wakefield, Leeds, Castle Vale Birmingham and New Cross.

New £300m bank facility arranged.

Net Assets at 31 March 2000	**£3,450m**

2001

Joint venture formed with London & Henley to own a portfolio of 758 apartments, mostly in Central London.

22 Homebase stores acquired – 865,000 sq ft of retail space.

Vicinitee established, a community and building management website.

A fibre optic loop and service centre for the Meadowhall Centre installed.

The Business Group set up to pursue opportunities in e-commerce.

British Land sells a 50% interest in 1 Fleet Place, 10 Fleet Place, 100 New Bridge St and Watling House into a joint venture with WestLB.

British Land attempts to acquire ordinary shares in Liberty International which, together with the Liberty shares already owned, would have given BL a 29.9% holding.

BL Fraser purchase Bentalls store in Bristol for £15.6m. BL Fraser lease the store to House of Fraser for £1.2m p.a. The acquisition is partly funded by a non-recourse bank loan, with the balance made up equally by BL and House of Fraser.

Agreement to subscribe for 50% of ordinary shares and loan stock in London & Henley Holdings for £18m as a joint venture to extend residential holdings of the company.

New 50:50 joint venture with Gazeley Properties created to purchase and develop 80 acres of distribution and industrial land at Colthrop Mill, Thatcham and Ravensbank Business Park, Redditch. It is anticipated the sites will have a combined end development worth of £120m.

8 acres of prime business land purchased at Clearwater Business Park, Theale for £15.25m.

Agreement in principle that Irish Life will acquire 73% of St Stephen's Green Shopping Centre, Dublin. BL will acquire 40% of the freehold of the Ilac Centre, Dublin with 40% being held by Irish Life and 20% by the Electricity Supply Board.

BL Universal sell 81 high street shops for £113m, continuing portfolio rationalisation begun in 1997.

Credit Lyonnais, Danske Bank and The Royal Bank of Scotland jointly arrange a £240m 5-year unsecured committed revolving credit facility.

Net Assets at 31 March 2001	£3,914m

2002

6.5% convertible bonds 2007 are redeemed.

A £575m securitisation of 35 Sainsbury stores and an £825m securitisation of the Meadowhall Centre are arranged.

At Regent's Place the HQ building for Abbey National is completed.

British Land's first CSR Report (Corporate Social Responsibility) is published.

Purchase of 22 Homebase stores from Sainsbury's for £156m at a yield of 7%.

Bondholders approve proposals to purchase the 2016 unsecured bonds and the 2023 bonds.

BL Davidson, the joint venture formed by the Davidson shareholders and Union Property Holdings (London), make a cash offer to acquire all of the issued and to be issued share capital of Asda not already contracted to be acquired by BL Davidson. BL Davidson end up with 51.34% of the current issued share capital by Asda.

375,000 sq ft at Plantation Place pre-let to Accenture at £54 per sq ft.

£125m profitable sales of properties made. The properties are Temple Court, Birmingham; Kingsthorpe Shopping Centre, Northampton; Connswater Centre, Belfast; and Bow Street Mall, Lisburn.

Forward purchase of 200,000 sq ft of A1 non-food retail and leisure accommodation at Orbital Shopping Park, near Swindon for £50m from ASDA Wal-mart. Previous to the transaction, ASDA Wal-mart secured pre-lets on 75% of the accommodation to major retailers Homebase, Comet, Next and JJB Sports.

Boldswitch enters into put and call arrangements in respect of its holding of 2,390,141 ordinary share in Haslemere NV.

Net Assets at 31 March 2002	£4,108m

2003

The European Bank for Reconstruction and Redevelopment agrees to remain at Broadgate until 2022.

Purchase of 1 Appold Street completes the Broadgate site of 4m sq ft on 34 acres.

British Land's share of Cherrywood is sold.

All properties in BL Rank are realised.

The development of Centre West, the extension to the Plaza Centre in East Kilbride, is completed.

The ARC is launched at Meadowhall. This will enable retailers to consolidate storage, reduce delivery costs and improve stock replenishment and visibility via a data link from store to warehouse. A joint venture is formed with Comgenic to sell the sytem to other shopping centre operators in the UK and abroad.

British Land continues to take an active position in PISCES, PropEX and HighSpeed Office (HSO).

London and Henley Holdings sells 3 properties containing 135 apartments for £31m. A number of medium term leases on the remaining properties in the London & Henley Holdings portfolio are entered into which earns £4.5m or 43% p.a. of the total rent roll of this portfolio.

Purchase of 5 freehold sites totalling 43.7 acres adjacent to Sheffield's Meadowhall Centre for £13.75m.

Acquisition of the other 50% of Broadgate Phase 12, the company undertaking the development of 201 Bishopsgate, from Railtrack for £40.25m.

Acquisition of Meadowbank Retail Park, Edinburgh for £30m.

BL Gazeley completes major transactions: contract to sell on completion a distribution facility at Mill Park, Thatcham to Matrix Securities; pre-let taken by MacFarlane Group at Delta Park, Enfield; Warburtons purchase 3.72 acres at Delta Park; a speculatively built warehouse at Delta Park is let to Powwow; and 2.23 acre site at Ravensbank Business Park, Redditch sold to Shepherd Developments.

Major lettings at the Meadowhall Centre to Zara, USC, Sports Soccer, Schuh, Van Heusen, Quiksilver, and Monserrat. Rental income is increased by £2m p.a.

FRP Group accept recommended cash offers with a loan note alternative from Union Property Holdings London for the whole of the issued and to be issued share capital of the group.

47,000 sq ft of office space let at Regent's Place to Elexon and Capital One.

| Net Assets at 31 March 2003 | £4,123m |

2004

The development of Plantation Place is completed. 10 Exchange Square also completed.

Heads of terms are agreed for the 465,000 sq ft pre-let with Willis for a London HQ at 51 Lime Street, on the site of the old Lloyd's of London building.

British Land buys out its partner, GUS, in the BLU joint venture.

Blythe Valley Park in Solihull is completely taken over from the joint venture partners ProLogis.

The Scottish Retail Property Limited Partnership is formed with Land Securities, pooling shopping centre interests in East Kilbride and Aberdeen.

British Land takes a 15.8% participation in the Songbird Consortium which owns 60.8% of Canary Wharf.

350 units (mostly flats) are purchased, or agreed on, for £60m from known housebuilders prior to completion.

New mutually advantageous covenants are introduced with principal banks.

£98m is raised through US Private Placement.

The Meadowhall and Werretown (Sainsbury) securitisations are both tapped to raise an additional £51m and £84m respectively.

Broadgate Estates Limited continues to grow. 60% of its income is earned from third parties.

BL Gazeley sells Enfield Distribution Park for £25.25m to Legal & General with a net initial yield of 7%. The sale is concluded within days of completion of the final warehouse unit.

Firmount agree to sell its remaining 27% interest in St Stephen's Green Shopping Centre for Euro64m to a leading Irish investor.

Werretown Supermarkets Securitisation, a special purpose vehicle, issues further bonds to extend the existing securitisation of 35 supermarkets owned by the British Land Group and let to J Sainsbury.

Net Assets at 31 March 2004	£4,669m

2005

The limited partnership BL Rosemound secures a pre-letting to EXCEL Logistics for a 300,000 sq ft distribution warehouse facility at DIRFT.

Marconi Communications agree terms for the development of a new 310,000 sq ft HQ campus at New Century Park, Coventry, plus an 80,000 sq ft distribution unit.

Contracts exchanged for a transaction encompassing 23 freehold and long leasehold Debenhams retail properties – 3.28m sq ft of department stores for a value of £495m.

Completion of the £2.1 billion refinancing of the Broadgate Estate. As a result of this transaction, Broadgate Financing issues £2.080bn of bonds at an average interest rate of 5.05%. The weighted average maturity of the new bonds is 20 years.

Net Assets at 31 March 2005

£5,579m (IFRS £4,783m)*

2006

Purchase of five Homebase stores from Sainsbury's for £52m. With an area totaling 181,000 sq ft, these acquisitions are to be owned by British Land under new 150 year leases.

Acquisition of outstanding 50% interest in BL West Companies by buying for £50m shares owned by WestLB AG and others.

The BL Rosemound joint venture at DIRFT completes the sale of a 300,000 sq ft pre-let freehold distribution warehouse to Sun Life Unit Assurance Limited.

Acquisition of Pillar Property, adding its specialist team and £1.5bn of high quality open A1 retail parks and its fund management business (over £3bn under managment).

Firmount Limited and Arch Properties Limited sell a 50% interest in the Ilac Shopping Centre, Dublin for £121.32m.

Sale of 10 Fleet Place (part of the Ludgate Estate) to CIT for a gross price of £109.12 million.

Sale of interest in 2–16 Baker Street to McAleer & Rushe for £57.20m.

Sale of nine retail properties from High Street portfolio for a total of £52.25m.

Completion of the letting of 42,000 sq ft of the top three floors at Plantation Place South to the specialist insurer Beazley Group on a 15 year lease at rents of £43 and £44 per sq ft.

Sale of the 999 year lease of 1 Fleet Place for £119.5m to Legal & General following the restructure of the lease to Denton Wilde Sapte for 20 years without break at £36 per sq ft. Initial yield of 5%.

Sale of Heathrow Gateway, Feltham to New Star Property Unit Trust for £65m.

Sale of seven retail properties for a total sale

price of £137m., including Greyhound Retail Park, Chester; Priory Retail Park, Merton; four in-town Somerfield supermarkets and a prime shop in Donegall.

Sale of Legal & General House, Kingswood for £73.6m to Kingswood Property Holdings, with funding from The Royal Bank of Scotland.

Sale of £300m residential property investment portfolio to Insight Investment. BL contracts to provide on-going asset management services for the portfolio.

Refinancing of existing superstore portfolio reduces Group interest cost by £7m p.a. A new simplified securitisation issued by BL Superstores Finance is expected to amount to £750 million and includes £52 million in new floating rate bonds. The new financing is expected to have a weighted average interest rate of approximately 4.9%.

Sale of Auldhouse Retail Park, Glasgow for £39.8m to AXA REIM UK.

Sale of B&Q retail warehouse at Portrack Lane Teesside for £29.25m to DVS, yielding 4.64%.

Sale of part of the Plantation Place development for £527m to Tishman International and Clients of Insight Investment Management.

Purchase of Ropemaker Place EC2 for £130m.

Joint venture formed with Copcisa Corp to develop 1 million sq ft mixed retail and leisure scheme Puerto Venecia in Zaragoza, Spain.

Acquisition of Partner's share of BL Davidson for £253m. The investment portfolio consisting mainly of retail parks and London offices is valued over £700m.

Net Assets at 31 March 2006   £6,016m (IFRS)*

* Net Assets in the Balance Sheet under International Financial Reporting Standards.

Share Price Performance
1970 — Aug 2006

Source: UBS, Datastream

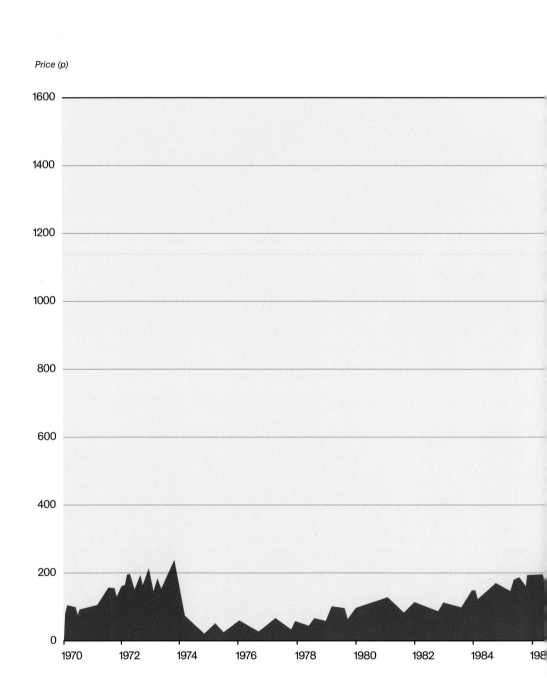

Price (p)

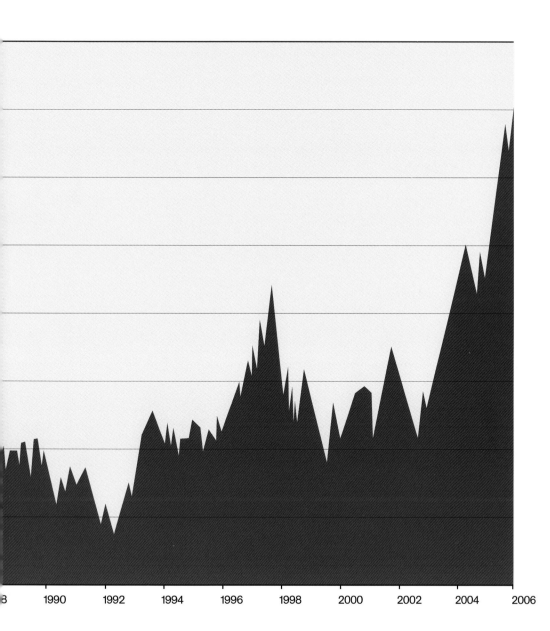

8   1990   1992   1994   1996   1998   2000   2002   2004   2006

Index